Building A Vision For Your Life

Discovering Your Core Motivator And Why It Matters

BOB PERKINS

WESTBOW
PRESS®
A DIVISION OF THOMAS NELSON
& ZONDERVAN

WestBow Press books may be ordered through booksellers or by contacting:

WestBow Press
A Division of Thomas Nelson & Zondervan
1663 Liberty Drive
Bloomington, IN 47403
www.westbowpress.com
844-714-3454

Scripture quotations are from the ESV Bible® (The Holy Bible, English Standard Version®), copyright © 2001 by Crossway Bibles, a publishing ministry of Good News Publishers. Used by permission. All rights reserved.

ISBN: 979-8-3850-3028-6 (sc)
ISBN: 979-8-3850-3029-3 (e)

Library of Congress Control Number: 2024916043

Print information available on the last page.

WestBow Press rev. date: 08/19/2024

Contents

IT'S TIME FOR BOB TO GO.

T he meeting was scheduled for four o'clock Monday afternoon at a hotel near the airport. I picked up my boss and took him to his room. There we met a coworker to discuss some problems the coworker and I were having. This had been billed as a meeting to resolve difficulties and to plan for the future. I knew this was going to be a difficult meeting. I might have to say some difficult things to this person, and I might also have to hear some tough things from him. I had been in these kinds of meetings before, and I was confident that, in the end, things would be worked out. I would get the promotion I had been promised just weeks prior to the meeting.

After about ten minutes, I realized from the tone of the meeting that the agenda and outcome had been set well in advance without my knowledge or participation. Instead of an attempt at reconciliation, the meeting was a rehearsed confrontation. I knew immediately I had been ambushed.

I turned to my boss and said, "You've come here to fire me."

He was caught off guard and stared at his feet for several minutes. When he finally spoke, he said, "That's one option." It was in fact his only option. Two hours later, he told my advisory board of directors, "It's time for Bob to go."

I was being pushed out! I felt betrayed. I had championed this coworker's career, and now he was trying to replace me. I was deeply hurt, angry, and afraid. I was thirty-nine years old and had been with the organization for thirteen years. By most measures, I had done very well. I had moved from my hometown to serve in two different locations. I had produced results, earned my master's degree, and grown the work of the organization in each of the areas I had served. From a success perspective, I was one of the top performers in the country, but the political winds had changed, and I was out.

At almost forty years old, with a family, mortgage, car payments, and credit card bills, my time was up, and I needed to find new work.

I loved my job, and I loved the organization for which I worked. I was successful at what I did. I had good friendships in the organization. Sure the last couple of years had been rough; change was brewing, but I believed the organization would see the value of keeping someone with my experience, wisdom, and success. I was deceiving myself. I had seen other senior staff pushed out, and I would be no different. This was a young man's game, and I wasn't getting any younger.

I had told myself that eventually, this would happen to me. I knew the odds were against being one of the few who would retire from this organization, yet emotionally, I didn't want to believe that I would be rejected. I didn't want to believe it could happen to me.

As I processed the coming transition, I resolved to learn from my mistakes and do things differently the next time around. I knew there would be plenty of time later to evaluate the previous thirteen years, but at that moment, I needed to figure out what I was going to do next. For the first time in a long time, I was looking for a job.

I didn't even know where to begin. I needed a job, but I didn't need just any job—I needed the right job. I needed the job that would be right for me, for who I am. I was too old to make a mistake with what would be the rest of my career. I found myself asking questions I hadn't asked for a long time, questions that seemed more appropriate for late-night fraternity house discussions but which were as real now (maybe more so) as they had been during those late-night college bull sessions.

I began trying to figure out who I was and what I should be doing with my life.

I realized that the biggest threats I faced were emotional, and I knew I couldn't let myself slide into depression. I wasn't only losing a job—after more than twenty years of being involved with the organization—I was losing a family, too. The people in the organization, those on the team, had become like family to me. One of the first lessons I learned was that my attachment to the organization was unhealthy. I had found my identity in belonging to the organization and had lost the essence of who I was; I no longer knew the real me. I knew I had to rediscover who I was if I was ever going to be healthy again.

But other questions loomed.

1. *If I don't find my significance, value, and worth in this or any other job, then where will I find them?*
2. *How will I go about finding out what is the right work for me?*
3. *If I can't trust a good organization like this, then whom can I trust?*
4. *How will I discover who I am?*

The first principle I learned was that to build a new vision for my life or to create for the first time a vision for my life, I needed to look at something more meaningful than the next great job. I needed to look beyond the salary, the benefits, and the retirement plan. I needed to build my life on a more solid foundation—the foundation of who I am and who I have been created to be. This first principle is the key to creating a *Vision for Your Life* and the beginning of the process.

This book is about what I discovered in the process of working through these dramatic changes in my life. It is about plotting a vision for your life and doing the work that is the right work for you—the unique individual that is you.

The first and perhaps the most important concept in this work is this, I do not begin with the premise that something is wrong with you that needs to be fixed. I am not going to tell you that if you change X or do *this* better or *that* more efficiently, you will have a successful life. That is the *know-who-you-aren't-and-fix-it* paradigm, and I reject that.

The concepts discussed in the *Vision for Your Life* process are powerful because they begin and end with the premise that God made every human being uniquely and wonderfully. The philosophy here is not to "know who you aren't and fix it" but rather *"know who you are and be it."*

PRINCIPLE 1: KNOW WHO YOU ARE AND BE IT, NOT KNOW WHO YOU AREN'T, AND FIX IT.

This book will deal with that which is deepest inside of us. I will not be discussing your personality traits or your gifts and skills. There is an appropriate place for a discussion of personality, and there are many other fine books written on that subject. This book will look at what is deeper than personality and what is core to who you are. This isn't about what skills you've learned over the course of your life. This is not a book about how to build a resume. There are many good books already written about that as well, rather it is about who you *are*.

In one sense, I want to reset the stage and reimagine how we think about our lives and the work we do. To set a vision for our lives, we must understand *who* we are before we think about where we want to go. In other words, the vision for our lives begins with gaining a clear picture of who we are as unique individuals and celebrating that uniqueness with the totality of our lives. I call this process *visioneering.*

I invite you to celebrate the unique person God made you to be and to gain a clear picture of what a full life can look like.

BEFORE WE BEGIN, I want to make it clear that it is my contention that the principles put forth in this book will hold true for anyone, whatever his or her belief system is. This book is written from a Christian perspective. It is grounded in the perspective that the Bible is true and that God became a man in the person of Jesus Christ. But essential truths—what Francis Schaeffer called true truths—are valid for every person in the same way that gravity is true for every person, regardless of one's particular belief in God.

For example, while you and I will agree that gravity exists, we may not agree as to how it was created. In the same way, I believe that God created us as unique individuals, we do not have to embrace the same view of creation for us to agree that each of us is unique. In this way, the principles in this book hold true—like the law of gravity—regardless of where we believe these principles originated.

This book is written for all of us. While the genesis of the ideas put forth in this book came from my own experience, the principles are true no matter what your situation. Perhaps you are well satisfied with the path you are on. You are fulfilled in your career, secure in your relationships, and wake up each day with a general sense of contentment. The principles in this book will help you gain a clearer picture of who you are and the direction in which your life can go.

Or perhaps you are not fully satisfied with your life. Perhaps you have been going along, doing what seemed to be the right things, but life hasn't worked out the way you planned. You may have received a good education, landed a great job, married a wonderful person, and have awesome kids. Now, however, your life has been turned upside down. You wonder what went wrong and how to rebuild your life. This book is for those of you caught in that situation, too.

Vision for Your Life was originally developed for middle-aged baby boomers in crisis. To my pleasant surprise, I've seen the principles outlined here resonate with people of all ages and in all places in life. As I've worked with clients from college kids to senior citizens, helping them to "build a vision for their life," I've come to realize that this process is for those who are just beginning on the journey of life as well as those who have already traveled far along the path of life.

It is particularly exciting and encouraging to see people getting a *vision for their life* in their twenties and thirties, well before they hit a midlife crisis. If this is you, I trust that what you read here will give you a clear sense of who you are and enable you to build clear pictures of what your life can look like when lived to the fullest.

This book is also for those of you who think that life has nearly passed you by—who think it's too late to find significance in life and be energized by the work you do. It is for all of us who were created in the image of God and meant to live life to the fullest.

Thanks for taking the time to read this book and for making the investment in this process of discovering a *Vision for Your Life*.

Acknowledgments

A great number of people have been helpful to me in writing this book. It would be impossible to thank everyone who has done so, but I would like to highlight a few friends who have helped make this possible.

My sister Debbie, who spent a week with me organizing this book. We put all of the major thoughts, illustrations, and theology on large pieces of paper and hung them around her dining room. She helped me see the component parts and put my thoughts in order. She was my dear friend and biggest fan. She passed at far too young an age (fifty-two), and I think of her every day.

My mom, who modeled the priority of relationships every day of her life, and my dad, to whom I owe honesty, wisdom, and insight. My brother and sister, whom I love deeply.

My mentors—Jerry Johnson, who taught me the blocking and tackling of leadership and gave us plenty of laughs; Paul Kooistra, who patiently walked with me and helped me understand reformed theology in practice and leadership; Jerram Barrs, who was willing to sit with me for hours upon hours and discuss the application of God's grace and truth in every situation; Hal Merwald, who cared for me when I was damaged goods and taught me to see the world from another perspective, thank you.

My many clients who have believed in me and in the *Vision for Your Life* process—I wouldn't understand anything *about Core*

Motivators if some of you hadn't been willing to be *guinea pigs* when this all first started, thank you.

To Eric Herrenkohl, who told me, "That's not your *Core Motivator*," and started the whole discussion. Thank you.

To Andy Parham, who has believed in this work and has been committed to its development. Thank you.

To the coaches who have come along for this ride—Theron Huff, Eric Johnson, Mike Sambrook, and Naa Yirinki, thank you.

Most of all, to my wife, Debbie, and my boys, Bryan and Taylor—I am a blessed man to have such a fabulous family. Deb is the rock that has stood firm through all the ups and downs. She believes in me and challenges me, follows me, and loves me—I am eternally grateful for her steadfast faith and love. Bryan and Taylor, you have brought me more joy than any father deserves. I love you both.

Jesus—He loves me, this I know because the Bible tells me so. I am weak, but He is strong. Thank you!

Why a second edition?

It has been over ten years since the first edition was published, and we have learned a lot about *Core Motivators* in that time. The number of people who have gone through the *Core Motivator* process has expanded exponentially, and it seemed time to update this book with the new information.

Much of what we knew in 2013 hasn't changed. The concept and understanding of *Core Motivators* have mostly stayed the same. But we have grown in a much deeper understanding of each of the *Core Motivators*, and we want to share that additional understanding with you here.

Introduction

TELL ME ABOUT THIS VISION THING

V ision is seeing. The *Merriam-Webster Dictionary* defines vision as "that act or power of imagination, mode of seeing or conceiving, a picture of the future."

When you look at your life, what are the pictures you see? What images stir in your imagination when you think about your future? *Vision for Your Life* is about defining the pictures we have for our lives—pictures that encompass the essence of who we are and what we do with our days—the areas where we need vision the most.

Without a vision for our lives, we either live someone else's vision or we wander aimlessly. If we don't have a vision that is built on our own core, then we tend to adopt a vision given to us by someone else, or we simply muddle along without direction.

Perhaps you had a high school coach or teacher who in a casual moment said, "I think you would make a great teacher." Then for lack of any other direction, you became a teacher. Or perhaps your parents always told you to be a doctor, and one day you found yourself in medical school even though you didn't know if it was right for you. You were simply there because your folks told you they thought you should do it. That's "living someone else's vision." The vision didn't come from a focused effort to know who you are; it was from someone else's suggestion.

The only thing worse than following someone else's vision for our lives is to wander aimlessly. Without any vision, we simply go from job to job, person to person, and group to group and never have a clear direction for our lives. True vision is more than the next job, the next relationship, or the next group. Vision is the overall picture of your life that gives you clear direction for what you will do with your life based on who you are.

The goal of this book is to provide you with the specific framework needed to guide you through the process of building a vision for your life. It begins with the unique premise, "know who you are and be it," and bases the picture(s) you develop on the idea of a congruent life that aligns your skills, personality, gifts, and *Core Motivator*.

In this book, we will discuss how you

1. *discover your Core Motivator,*
2. *set a star or personal vision statement,*
3. *establish mountains or benchmarks, and*
4. *identify tools to navigate your mountains.*

Two Dangers

Danger 1

There are two potential dangers associated with *visioneering*. The first arises almost every time I speak to a group about *Vision for Your Life*. Although the question is not always framed identically, it is always asked in some form or another. "What if my vision for my life is to go off and join the circus? I can't just abandon the responsibilities I have to my family."

It is true that you can't abandon your responsibilities, but it's also true that the circus is a job, not a vision for your life. Changing jobs may indeed be the result of this process, but it may also be that you will continue in your present career in a more energized way.

The question points to the crux of the problem. We tend to view our lives through the primary lens of our jobs instead of viewing our jobs in the context of the greater vision of our lives.

The real question is "Is the life you are leading now—including your job—truly an outflow of who you are and who you were created to be?" As you discover who you are, your circumstances may or may not have to change, but it is always better to be wholly you in a different job than to be half, or less, of who you are in your present job. As you develop a total vision for your life, you will have a new perspective on your life and your work that will enable you to be more of the person God created you to be.

Danger 2

The second danger associated with visioneering is the problem of shooting at a moving target. If we begin our thinking from the viewpoint of what we think is important today, we may be dealing with a moving target. What we want now may not be what we'll want five or ten years down the road—not to mention what we'll want for the rest of our lives. Our wants and desires are constantly changing.

I remember when all I wanted was a good job and a fast car. Then I wanted a good job that made lots of money, a fast car, and a wonderful wife. Then I wanted a great job, a reliable car, a wonderful wife, and a big house. I won't tell you what I want now, but fortunately I still have a wonderful wife! Do you remember what you wanted out of life when you graduated from college? How many times has that changed between then and now?

Good navigation—like any well-planned journey—begins with a clear vision of the starting point, the end point, and the path that the journey must take. When life planning starts with an arbitrary starting point—in this case, temporary wants, or desires (a big house, fancy car, or country club membership) instead of a vision for the whole journey—then it is doomed to fail because it ultimately does not satisfy our deepest questions or needs. We're starting at the wrong place and aiming for the wrong end. If we don't have the right beginning and end points, then we'll certainly end up on the wrong path. Finding the right starting point and end point is essential in plotting the correct path for our lives.

This book is therefore divided into two sections. The first sections—chapters 1–5—are an assessment of the cultural attitudes and philosophy that most of us have followed which have given us the context for our lives today.

The second section of this book is a look at the process of discovering your *Core Motivator* and plotting a *Vision for Your Life*.

Chapter 1

THE PROBLEM

B efore discussing why and how we must think differently about our lives, it might be good to look at where we are and how we got here. I mean, how did our current society get to the place of thinking the way we do about life?

Most of us have built our lives on an existing set of assumptions (or paradigms) that have been passed down from one generation to the next with little change. We want to do well in life. We want to have the good things and experiences of life. We've based our lives on the virtues of education, hard work, family, community, and so on—all good principles. Those virtues were the fabric of a relatively stable post–World War II society, and while we adopted many of those principles for ourselves, the underlying justification for those principles has been challenged by subsequent generations.

In areas such as marriage, substance abuse, church attendance, work, and materialism, the justification of the old ways just didn't cut it.

Part of the rebellion of the baby boomers in the 1960s was a reaction to this sense of a lost philosophical basis for living. We wanted deeper answers to the question of *why* when we challenged all the existing paradigms. A culture that faced the Great Depression and a world war asked, "Will I have enough money to eat?" and

"Will the world survive?" They didn't have the luxury of being able to worry about the meaning of life.

Baby boomers were born in a nation of prosperity. They challenged the established institutions—the church, the government, and the family—to give a deep-rooted justification for their beliefs, laws, and traditions. When those justifications proved inadequate, they rejected them outright and created new realities. As a result, the world changed a great deal.

With the technology revolution, the emergence of the internet, our addiction to our phones, and the experience of COVID-19, the world has changed dramatically again, and not one area of our lives has been left untouched by those changes.

The principles sufficient for the previous generations now lack the sufficient deeper philosophical underpinning needed to sustain the dramatic changes that have occurred in our society. It is as if our lives had been held together by philosophical duct tape, and the holes couldn't be patched anymore, so society began to unravel.

The way we engage our work has completely changed. The idea of working for one company or organization for an entire career is unlikely to be realized. It is doubtful that many of us will stay with one organization for more than ten years, and we will probably never get a gold watch for fifty years of service with one organization. In our world today, we live on the edge of being out of work at any moment. In the current economic environment, organizations are constantly downsizing in an attempt to become more cost-effective. Organizations are looking to be lean and mean, and the loyalty of a company to a person is a thing of the forgotten past. In turn, personal loyalty to a company is also rare, as individuals are on a constant quest for a better job with a bigger salary, more benefits, and greater personal flexibility. We are a culture of individuals looking out for number one.

Although we no longer have the old institutions and societal structures to help define our lives, we also have not found adequate replacements for those paradigms we rejected.

We are more lonely, empty, and depressed than any generation before us while more affluent and materialistic than any generation before us. We long for a sense of community and connection with other people, and we want significance in our work. Yet we continue to act in ways that make us more isolated and continue to focus on the monetary benefits as almost the only measure of evaluating our lives.

We buy bigger houses that are farther apart from each other, and we are suspicious of any organization that asks us to join. The generations before us joined clubs—Masons, Lions, Elks, and Rotary—where people engaged one another relationally. Today we join country clubs or gyms where we exchange niceties with other members but lack a sense of connection and community.

It may have been right to question and reject the shallowness of the old institutions, but we have replaced them with materialism and isolation and now live with the consequences. What we need is a new way of looking at our lives, one that has a deep and solid foundation that will not crack when challenged.

Creation itself provides us with such a foundation. Our unique creation as individuals is a strong enough foundation on which to build lives of fulfilled significance, purpose, and meaning. Such lives will build strong communities where each person understands his or her value, purpose, and significance as part of the greater fabric of God's creation.

We need to write a new *play of life* based on who we are, not simply the rehearsed lines of the plot we were born into.

The Play of Life

Let me give an illustration of what I am talking about when I speak of the play of life. A theater critic once stated that there are basically two different types of productions—those that are plot-driven and those that are character-driven. In a plot-driven play, the story is the most important element. This would be typical of a murder mystery or suspense thriller. An Agatha Christie play is captivating because we are interested in finding out *who* the killer is or *how* the murder was accomplished. The characters can be thinly drawn because they exist only to sustain and carry the plot. In the end, we don't care about the depth of the characters; we are only interested in finding out which one committed the crime.

In a character-driven play, however, the plot is of less importance than the characters. The plot exists to showcase the depth of the characters and their development through the telling of the story. The plot serves the character, not the other way around. In a play such as *Death of a Salesman* or a movie such as *Good Will Hunting,* we are not primarily concerned with the plot. Our focus is not on how much Willie Loman sells or what kind of job Will Hunting gets. Rather these dramas focus on the development of the characters over time. We are drawn into the characters' lives, and we sense their struggle, pain, victory, or defeat—which defines to a greater depth the characters we have come to care about. We may even see some of ourselves in a character and identify with him or her. We are drawn to look at our own lives more closely and explore our inner being more deeply.

In our culture, we live essentially plot-driven lives. The plot has been written, and we play our parts to make the story complete. The plot goes something like this, we get an education, find a good job, get married, buy a house, have kids, buy a bigger house, move up the corporate and social ladders, see our children enter into the same *play*, have grandchildren, and retire. At some point, we die. That is the plot-driven life, and we are actors on the stage, merely playing our roles to fulfill the plot.

But what would your life look like if you lived a character-driven life? In a character-driven life, your story would begin with the character—you, the person—not the plot. You would look at the person God created—the character you are—and develop your life based on that character. In a character-driven life, the plot serves the character, not the other way around.

The character is everything in this play, and we must focus on the development of the character to make the play (our lives) worth living. In this way, each of our lives will be different and vital because our lives will be based on the uniqueness of who God made us to be. The main character in the play of your life is you.

Most of us never stop long enough to look inside ourselves and ask these questions:

1. Who am I?
2. Who is this person that God has created with unique talents, gifts, and motivations?
3. What exists at the very core of who I am that motivates me to do all that I do in my life?
4. When God created me, whom did He create?
5. Who am I, and why am I unique?
6. Who is the character that is me?

To answer these questions, we must embark on a journey—a journey of discovering who we are in order to build a vision for our lives.

Chapter 2

CHANGING THE PARADIGM OF PURPOSE

Swing the bat!

I n my consulting practice, I am continually struck by the number
of people I meet who have no sense of purpose or passion in their
lives. Before going any further with a discussion of building a vision
for our lives, I believe it is appropriate to first look at the issues of
our purpose in life (this chapter) and our passion for living (the next
chapter).

The purpose of life is to be fully the people we were created to
be, and in order to be those people, we have to swing the bat.

Both of my sons played Little League baseball. It was supposed
to be fun. When my oldest, Bryan, was nine years old, his coach
encouraged him to take walks, get hit by the pitch, and bunt. I was
appalled. At nine years old, the goal is to learn the basics of baseball
and fall in love with the game. Kids should be learning to field,
catch, throw, and hit the baseball. You don't learn to hit a baseball
by taking walks and getting hit by the pitch, and you will never fall
in love with the game by constantly being *beaned*. You learn the art
of hitting by swinging the bat.

Of course, you will strike out a lot if you swing the bat (let's
not forget that Babe Ruth was not only a home run king but also
a strikeout king). But if you don't swing the bat, you can never hit

the ball. The key to becoming a good hitter and enjoying baseball is to swing the bat. You must learn what strikes look like, which pitches to swing at, and which pitches to let pass into the catcher's mitt for called balls. That experience takes time, patience, and lots of swinging the bat.

At the beginning of the season, I developed one rule with my son. When we got home after a game, I would only be displeased if he hadn't swung the bat. I vowed never to criticize him for striking out or even for taking a walk if there weren't any good pitches to swing at (and I am a firm believer in the *earned walk*). My only criticism came when he did not swing the bat. A called third strike was the greatest baseball sin in our house.

At the beginning of the season, my son struck out a lot, and I was the least-liked parent on the team. That was OK because I was glad my son was swinging the bat. By midseason, guess who became the best hitter on the team? My son knew the thrill of hitting doubles and triples. While the other kids were still looking for walks, he was hitting the baseball. He experienced the joy of being the big hitter on the team, scoring the winning run, and being cheered on by his teammates. He learned to hit the ball because he pushed through the failure of swinging the bat, and he developed a love of the game.

We all must learn to face the potential failures in our lives and swing the bat. Too many of us live without ever swinging the bat. We are looking for a walk in life, and then we are frustrated because we never get the opportunity to make the big hit in a clutch situation. We are driven by our fears instead of our confidence. When we should be living life to the maximum and swinging for the fences, we are letting belt-high pitches go by, hoping the umpire will give us a walk.

We are looking for what our parents will give us, what the government will give us, what our employers will give us, what our church will give us, or what our friends will give us. We have become a culture of people waiting for what will be given to us instead of taking risks, accepting failure, and learning to swing the bat.

In Puerto Rico, they have a saying among baseball players, "You can't walk off the island." In other words, you have to hit your way off the island. No major league scouts are looking for players with the most walks; they are looking for those with the most hits. The same is true in life. We can't walk our way out of mediocrity; we have to hit our way to fulfillment. *We have to swing the bat.*

To view this from a larger perspective, we need to understand that God did not create life to be bland or for us to be miserable. God created us to have a great life. It is not that life is to be easy or superficially happy, and I'm not talking about a *prosperity gospel* here. Rather God created us to enjoy life and to live it to the fullest.

In fact, Jesus said, "I have come that they might have life, and that they may have it more abundantly" (John 10:10). God's desire is for us to live abundant lives, and this is part of why Jesus came to earth. So why are we not living that kind of abundant life? Why are we afraid to swing the bat?

Could it be that most of us have a wrong view of what God desires for us? Have we somehow gotten the idea that God wants us to live a life of unpleasant dissatisfaction, sadistically watching as we suffer the pain of this life? Do we have the idea that God is out to spoil all our fun with His rules? When we experience fulfillment in life, do we think God is somehow unhappy? If so, then we need to understand that this view isn't based on the God revealed in the Bible. The God of the Bible says that He wants us to have abundant life!

What has happened to us? If God wants us to live abundant lives, then why do so few of us live that way? Why have so many of us settled for a half-life that is lived in the safe zone of little risk and few rewards? Why are we so prosperous yet so unfulfilled? Why is it that with all the material comforts, economic success, and relationship expertise in our world, so many of us are still unsatisfied with our lives? Why are the suicide rates so high (especially among young people), and why is the need for anti-depressant drugs so great? What is wrong with the way we look at life that makes us question the very purpose of our existence? Why has life lost its zest? What is wrong with this paradigm?

A friend's motto is "Life is too short to wear beige." That, in essence, is what I am talking about. Life is too short to be bland, ordinary, and complacent. The new paradigm I'm talking about in this book involves living life to its fullest and getting the most out of the years we have been given. It's about regrouping and redefining our lives. It is about defining our existence according to who we were created to be and living that life to the fullest. We are to live our days with the kind of kinetic energy that makes us vibrant and thrilling individuals.

The key to this kind of living is to spend our days with a clear vision for our lives, and a sense of the adventure that vision entails.

WHAT LIFE SHOULD LOOK LIKE

An elderly nun allegedly coined the phrase, "Don't *should* on me," but if you'll allow me for just a minute, I want to do some *shoulding*. We *should* be getting up in the morning *excited* about our day. We *should* be approaching our relationships with a sense of emotional health and excitement. We *should* be looking forward every day to the great things that await us in the next twenty-four hours, the next week, and the years ahead of us. We *should* know the essence of our inner being and who we were created to be. We *should* be constantly thrilled by the daily pursuit of our dreams.

Why don't most of us live this way? Why have we settled for a safe life instead of an exciting, passionate, and adventurous life? What keeps us from swinging for the fences?

The answer for too many of us is FEAR.

Most of us are defeated by our fears. We hold back from swinging the bat because we are afraid we might strike out—and we might. Fear is what keeps us from living the great life we were meant to live. To contextualize Tennyson, "It is better to have swung the bat and struck out than never to have swung at all." We need to get beyond our fears and stretch ourselves to the point where we are no longer afraid to swing the bat in our lives.

Let's continue with the baseball analogy. One of the frustrations of any Little League coach is to try to get kids to hit in a game the same way they hit in the batting cage. At the midweek practice, each kid gets his turn in the batting cage. They stand and face a machine throwing perfect pitches at about the same speed (or harder) than they will face in the real game. With nothing to lose, the kids swing at every pitch and generally hit the stitches off the ball.

When game time comes, those same kids stand in the batter's box afraid to swing the bat. The confidence that they could not fail in the batting cage has given way to the reality that they may possibly fail in front of their coaches, teammates, family, and friends. The fear of failure has paralyzed them. Conversely when my son knew that I wasn't going to be angry with him if he struck out, his fear of failure was gone; he was free to swing the bat.

The Bible says, "There is no fear in love; but perfect love casts out fear" (1 John 4:18). In other words, because God loves us, we have nothing to fear, and ultimately, we cannot fail in life. We will have struggles and challenges that may be difficult, but we cannot fail because nothing can separate us from the love of God.

The apostle Paul tells us in Romans 8:38, "For I am persuaded that neither death nor life, nor angels nor principalities nor powers, nor things present nor things to come, nor height nor depth, nor any other created thing, shall be able to separate us from the love of God which is in Christ Jesus our Lord." Nothing can separate us from the love of God—nothing. There is no failure, no strikeout, nothing. It may be hard to believe, but nothing we can do will separate us from the love of God.

For the person who believes in the Christian faith, this message is a great encouragement. Our fears can be put aside because God loves us, and nothing can separate us from His love.

But the principle that fear is our great enemy is a universal truth, regardless of anyone's belief system. Remember FDR's words: "The only thing we have to fear is fear itself."

Therefore, we must cast aside the fears that keep us from swinging the bat—from living life to the fullest. In other words, whether it's God's love or our observation of the realities of life, we must have the confidence to live a life of purpose and make the most of our lives by taking risks and swinging the bat.

What are you afraid of that is keeping you from living a life of God-inspired purpose? Make a list of those fears and begin to get honest with yourself. Are you afraid you will not have enough money? Are you afraid your marriage will end? Are you afraid your kids will not turn out the way you want? Are you afraid you'll die?

Which one of those fears is too much for God? Which one of those fears can you not trust God with?

Is your deepest fear that God doesn't love you enough to look out for you?

When we cast aside our fears, we are free to "swing the bat" and live the life of God-inspired purpose we were meant to live.

Chapter 3

LIVE A LIFE OF PASSION

C ould it be that so many of us are unfulfilled because we have never lived or worked out of our passion? Have we instead lived our lives out of what is safe? The first and most important paradigm shift in our thinking was to change the way we view our *purpose*. Now we must understand the need to live our lives out of our passion—a passion that is congruent with who we are.

The great artist Michelangelo lived his life out of who he was. Early in his career, he was asked by Pope Pius III to work on creating a grand tomb for the pope. After the artist had done some of the work, the pope removed Michelangelo from the project. The artist was not only deeply hurt but also believed the pope owed him money. A fight ensued, and Michelangelo left Rome in a huff and headed for Florence. After Pope Pius III died, the next pope, Julius II, asked Michelangelo to paint the Sistine Chapel. When Michelangelo said that he was still upset about the previous project, the new pope told him to simply put it out of his mind.

Michelangelo responded, "A man does not paint with his hands, he paints with his mind." I love that! Perhaps the greatest artist of all time knew that the talent wasn't in his hands—it was in his mind. Passion, like great art, begins in our minds.

WHAT WE THINK ABOUT IS WHAT WE BECOME, AND WHAT WE ARE
PASSIONATE ABOUT IS WHAT WE WILL DO.

Michelangelo lived the kind of life I'm talking about. His work was congruent with who he was, and he lived his life out of his passion for creating great art. He did not begin by deciding that being a sculptor was a good job and then trying to become one. He knew deep inside that he had to sculpt. It was in him. It was his passion. His life was defined by his passion, and his various jobs were built into his life.

His life was an adventure, and he died when he was eighty-nine years old, six days after finishing his last statue. When he was eighty-nine, he was still sculpting, still doing the difficult work of chiseling on marble because sculpting was not just his work—it was his passion and his life. His art flowed from the depth of who he was. He was living an abundant life and creating great art in his final days. What would it mean for each of us to live and work out of our passion?

PRINCIPLE 2: BUILD YOUR JOB INTO YOUR LIFE, NOT YOUR LIFE INTO
YOUR JOB

Most of us define our lives by thinking about our careers. We are asked at a young age, "What are you going to be when you grow up?" Our careers become the starting point for thinking about our lives. We define our jobs and then define the other elements of our lives. This is backward thinking.

Most of us have determined a career path, thought about how much education it will require, and then thought about when we would get married, have children, and begin to build our family lives. We even decide where we will live based on where our jobs take us. Our work has become the starting point for defining our lives, and if we are going to live lives of passion, then we must begin by changing that paradigm. We need a new starting point that begins not with what we will do, but rather with who we are.

When we were little kids, it would have been better if we had been asked, "How will you be *you* when you grow up?"

OUR PURPOSE AND PASSION SHOULD DEFINE OUR LIVES. WE SHOULD BUILD OUR JOBS INTO OUR LIVES INSTEAD OF OUR LIVES INTO OUR JOBS.

To live a life out of our purpose and passion, we are going to have to have a different view of work and retirement. In the next two chapters, I will address those issues and then turn to thinking about *Core Motivators*. For now, let's just say that our lives will be energized by purposeful and passionate work—the kind of work that is congruent with who we are and that sparks our passion. We may, at times, be tired *in* our work, but we will never be tired *of* our work.

We must think through the question, "What is my passion?" To help us gain an understanding of passion, let me give you two other examples (in addition to Michelangelo) of people who lived out of their passion and built their jobs into their lives, not their lives into their jobs: Cal Ripken Jr. and the Four Tops.

Cal Ripken Jr. may be the best shortstop to ever play the game (I grew up in Baltimore), but that is not why he will be forever remembered. Cal's place in baseball history is firmly entrenched because he broke Lou Gehrig's record for playing in the most consecutive games. Gehrig's record was 2,130 consecutive games, and Ripken's new record is 2,632. Think about that. Two thousand six hundred thirty-two days at work without ever missing a day. His name was on the starting lineup card two thousand six hundred and thirty-two times in a row.

Ripken loves baseball. He loved to play the game—it is part of who he is. When you watched Cal play, you knew that no one was making him come to the ballpark every day to do what he did. Cal was not grinding it out, and although he was paid very well for what he did, he was not doing it for the money. He was living his life fully.

In September 1997 the Orioles were in Toronto and had already been mathematically eliminated from the playoffs. Cal was playing third base (having been moved from shortstop the previous season), and a ball was hit down the third base line, just carrying over the base and curving into foul territory. Cal went six feet into foul territory to backhand the ball, planted his right foot, and threw a strike to first to get the batter out. It was an unbelievable play destined for the highlight reels. He did not have to give that kind of effort; his place in baseball history was already established. His team was out of the race for the season, but Cal Ripken couldn't play baseball any other way. He gave it his all every time he was on the field because he loved to play baseball, and he lived his life doing what he was passionate about. Although Cal entered the Baseball Hall of Fame, that honor was not his goal, it was the natural result of his living out of his passion.

GOALS NEVER GIVE YOU THE KIND OF PASSION REQUIRED TO ATTAIN GREATNESS. GREATNESS IS FULFILLED BY SIMPLY WORKING OUT OF OUR PASSION.

In addition to baseball, I love the Motown sound. In the sixties it was "the Sound of Young America," and my favorite group was the Four Tops. I have every album the Four Tops ever made, and I saw them perform more than twenty times. The Four Tops were together without personnel changes for over forty years, altering their lineup only when one of the members died. Charter members of the Rock 'n Roll Hall of Fame, they had many number one records. They helped define the Motown sound of the sixties and are arguably one of the greatest singing groups of all time. Their music—songs such as "I Can't Help Myself" (Sugar Pie Honey Bunch), "It's the Same Old Song," "Reach Out, I'll Be There," "Bernadette," and "Ain't No

Woman Like the One I've Got"—is still being played and enjoyed today.

The Tops loved to sing. They spent ten years on the Chitlin' Circuit performing in small clubs without a hit record prior to making it big. When other groups stopped singing as their careers fell on inevitable hard times, the Tops continued delighting audiences in small clubs, at private parties, or anywhere people would gather to hear them perform.

During their illustrious career, each of the members made the same amount of money. It was divided equally even though the lead singer Levi Stubbs could have demanded a disproportionate share of the proceeds. You see, these guys loved what they did, and they considered any opportunity to perform a privilege. Their lives were rich because they were passionate about what they did and were fortunate to be able to do what they were gifted for.

The last remaining member of the original Four Tops Abdul Fakir performed until he was eighty-eight years old. He continued to go out on stage, sometimes sitting on a stool, because it was his passion. He didn't need more money, and he didn't need more applause. He did it because he loved doing it.

Neither Cal Ripken nor the Four Tops ground out their lives in mundane existence. They defined their passion—baseball and singing—so that their lives reflected what they were passionate about. Their work was congruent with their passion, and they each swung the bat.

Most of us do not do what we are passionate about. We consider ourselves fortunate if we get to do something we like, but passionate work is a dream reserved for athletes, artists, and movie stars. Passionate work eludes average people like us. But we can live this kind of life.

The Four Tops and Cal Ripken had something else in common. Both continued to live in the cities in which they grew up. Cal Ripken grew up in Baltimore and still lives there. The Four Tops grew up in Detroit, and when the rest of Motown moved to California, they stayed. As much as they loved what they did, their lives were bigger than their careers. Show business (lest we forget, professional sports is show business too) was not the totality of their lives; it was only a part.

THEY BUILT THEIR JOBS INTO THEIR LIVES, NOT THEIR LIVES INTO THEIR JOBS.

Instead of defining all the elements in our life by our job, we should first define our life—our passionate and purposeful life—and then build *all* its various elements—our job, family, where we live, and so on—into that vision. We must think about our whole life as one where all the elements fit into a grand picture of who we are and where we are going.

When we begin to think about our lives by making all the elements of our lives fit into our jobs, we are often contorting ourselves into something other than who God created us to be, and we deceive ourselves. We think we have made ourselves more valuable when in reality we have missed the essence of our true value: unique creations of the God of the universe.

Chapter 4

CHANGING THE PARADIGM OF WORK

And when I run I feel His pleasure.
—Eric Liddell

In addition to misunderstanding the role of passion and purpose, we also tend to have a non-Biblical and detrimental view of work. We tend to see work as a necessary evil and something that makes our lives less enjoyable. We even believe that some work is more meaningful and significant than other work. In this chapter, I want to address those fallacies and present a Biblical view of work.

I was walking through an airport one day with my friend Jerram Barrs, talking about work. I was trying to make the point that some work has a higher value both in the eyes of God and in its contribution to society because it is of a higher social or spiritual value than other work. For example, the work of Mother Theresa is more valuable than the work of a guy balancing books or digging a ditch.

Jerram is one of the most intelligent people I've ever met, and he wasn't buying my premise. In frustration, I said to him, "I don't think you understand what I'm saying."

Jerram stopped, looked at me, and said, "Bob, I understand. I just don't agree." When Jerram doesn't agree with me, then I know I am wrong, and I was wrong. It took me a while, but I began to understand that all work is good, that work itself—the very activity of work—is good for us. Let me explain.

The movie, *Chariots of Fire*, is the true story of Eric Liddell, the son of missionaries in China, who won Olympic gold in the 1924 games in Paris. Eric was the fastest runner in Scotland and was torn between his desire to compete in the Olympics and his desire to return to the mission field in China. At a dramatic point in the movie, Eric tells his sister that he is going to return to the mission field, but first, he must run in the Olympics. When Eric sees the disappointment on his sister's face because she wants him to go directly to China, he explains to her, "God made me fast, and when I run, I feel His pleasure."

Liddell puts his finger on the issue. When we do what God has created us to do, then we feel His pleasure, and we are energized. That work is a good thing. The work itself is good. We must ask ourselves, "What is it in our lives that when we do that thing—that which God has created us to do—we feel His pleasure? What is the work we do that causes us to feel His pleasure?"

Work itself is of central importance in the process of building a vision for our lives. While we don't want to build our lives into our jobs, we still must consider the work we will do and the importance it will have in our lives. When we have the right understanding of work and where it fits in our lives, we will be solving a major piece of the puzzle, which is the vision for our lives.

It is important for us to think about the role of work in our lives because not only will we spend most of our waking hours working, but it is also important to recognize that God created us to work. And if God created us to work, it is, therefore, inherently good for us.

I believe that God created us to do meaningful and productive work, and for this reason, we must understand the importance of work from God's perspective.

Most of us are surprised to hear that God created us to work, and that work is inherently good for us. In our culture, we have made work a necessary evil, adopting the belief that we work only to attain the wants and needs in our lives. We tend to think that the work we do only provides us with a paycheck and the ability to purchase the things we want. We have confused the monetary rewards of work with the inherent value of work itself. This is a dangerous misunderstanding because when work is reduced to only a means to a monetary end, it loses its joy and value.

We must make a distinction between money and work. Money is the means by which we can purchase the goods, services, and experiences we desire. Work is the expenditure of energy, and it is good for us to expend energy because this is how we are constructed; it is part of how we were created by God. While the love of money may be a root of evil, work in and of itself is good!

Three points are important to consider when looking at the value of work. First we can see that God worked when He created the world; therefore, it is a good and holy activity. Second we can see that God gave man work to do in the Garden of Eden prior to the fall of man, and third we can see that when we are doing the kind of work that energizes us, we feel more alive than in any other activity.

To see that work is a good thing, let us begin by looking at the work God did in creating the world. The Bible describes God's creation activity as work. God himself performed work when he created the world, therefore, making work holy. As we look at those first chapters in Genesis, we see God working. God is a creator God, an active God, not a passive and lazy God. The Bible uses the Hebrew word for work (melachah) when speaking of God's own creative work. In Genesis 2, we are told that God rested from his work. Work, therefore, is a holy activity because God worked, and any activity of God is a holy activity because He cannot do anything that is outside of His holy nature.

Next we see that God gave man work to do in the Garden of Eden. We can see that before any evil was in the world—before there was sin—God shared His holy activity by giving man work to do in the Garden of Eden.

When we want to get a glimpse of the way God perfectly created man, we can look at the Garden of Eden and view life before man's fall into sin. We can even get a glimpse of heaven by looking at the garden because there we see the perfect, sinless world where God and humans cohabited perfectly. When we view life in the Garden of Eden, we see two important facts concerning work.

First Genesis 1:26 tells us, "Then God said, 'Let Us make man in Our image, according to Our likeness." Genesis 1:27 says, "So God created man in His own image." Humankind was created in the image of God, and part of that image-bearing was to be creatures who worked.

Second God created work for man before man fell into sin. God gave Adam a job to do in the garden. He told Adam to name the animals, and the naming process was Adam's work. Interestingly while God gave Adam the job of naming the animals, He did not tell Adam what to name them; this creative work was left to the man. This makes sense—this creative work reflected the nature and image of God and was embedded in the first humans. And this work was important to the first humans, just like it is important to us. So much of our own significance is attached to our work that we can intuitively understand why God gave man work to do in the garden. He knew (because He had created them in His image) that they needed significant work because it was essential to their being all of who they were. Adam and Eve found their significance in their relationship to God and in their work.

But there was more to work in the garden. Many of us in our current culture have the false impression that before humanity fell into sin, men and women did not have to perform any work. We think that their food just appeared out of the earth or dropped from the trees. Potatoes and carrots simply popped out of the ground on their own, ready to be eaten. We forget that although sin made the tasks difficult, the tasks themselves were always there.

Before sin entered the garden, work was enjoyable and painless, but after sin entered the world, there was pain in the labor of man's work. Likewise, prior to sin entering the world, women would still have gone into labor, but the curse of sin meant that from that moment forward, childbirth would be painful and not always successful. In this context, work was not God's punishment upon Adam; it was part of His perfectly created life for Adam even before the fall. Work was part of paradise!

Third we see that aside from providing Adam and Eve with significant work, God gave them a creative outlet for their time that would energize them and excite them about the next day. Can you imagine what life would have been like in the Garden of Eden if there had not been any work? What would Adam and Eve have done with their time? Lying in a hammock all day has its limits! It was a gift from God that mankind had the opportunity to spend his life in significant work.

To summarize, we can see that work is a holy activity because God worked, that He gave Adam and Eve work to do in the garden, and that the right work energizes us. Therefore, we must view work as a holy activity and as part of the nature of God that is instilled in every human being. When work is practiced in the context of godly obedience, it is an act of worship because it honors and glorifies God. When work is performed for motives other than honoring God, it becomes an act of idolatry because the aim becomes self-aggrandizement or simply the acquisition of money for self-satisfaction.

Work is an intricate part of our makeup. Work is good for us—good for our overall well-being mentally, emotionally, and physically—and is as essential to our well-being as eating, breathing, and sleeping. Conversely when we are not working or when we are doing the wrong work, it is detrimental to our well-being. Without work, our minds and bodies become weak, and we move into a lazy and depressed state. The challenge for us is to find the right work.

Work and the Industrial Revolution

The impact of the Industrial Revolution on our view of work cannot be understated. Prior to the Industrial Revolution, people generally worked together on a farm or in a small shop as a family unit. After the Industrial Revolution, the family no longer worked together toward a common goal. The man left home every day and went to the factory to earn wages, apart from his family.

The nature of man's work changed too. No longer was he part of the creating process from beginning to end as he had been prior to the Industrial Revolution. On the farm, he had been involved in tilling the soil, planting the seeds, and nurturing and harvesting the crops. In the shop, he had been involved in the buying, marketing, and selling of his goods. He had been intimately involved in the whole process.

When his job moved to the factory, he saw only the specific part of the manufacturing process in which he was involved. He became just another cog in the wheel of production instead of the creator of a complete project.

The consequences of this paradigm shift were felt in every part of society. The family no longer had a father present in the house all day long, and the provider of sustenance was no longer God—via sun and rain for the crops—but the company and the government. After this paradigm shift, work itself changed for many. No longer did work have the same significance and meaning. Instead it became merely a means to an end, the avenue to earn money in order to purchase things that would make life better.

Now don't misunderstand me. I'm not suggesting that the Industrial Revolution was a bad thing or that we should all move to Lancaster County in Pennsylvania and live a technology-free existence, like the Amish. I'm simply saying that we need to recognize what changed. The Industrial Revolution brought prosperity to a mass of people who would have never known it, but we must separate the activity of the revolution from the consequences of it. We must change the philosophical paradigm that was a byproduct of the Industrial Revolution and again see work as a good thing.

The technological revolution has again changed the way we think about work. Instead of mindless work on a factory floor, we are mindfully engaged behind a computer screen. The circumstances have changed, but the difficulty in finding meaning in our work continues.

We must embrace our work with the same kind of passion that guided generations before us and inspired people like Cal Ripken, the Four Tops, and Eric Liddell.

ANOTHER LOOK AT ERIC LIDDELL

Running was the work that Eric Liddell had to do; the work (passion) God gave to him. When he ran, he felt God's pleasure. If we think back on our lives, most of us have experienced a time when we couldn't wait to get up in the morning to go to work. We've known—if only for a short period of time—the thrill that comes with doing some form of work we love. We all have work to do that energizes us in a way that when we do it, we feel God's pleasure.

How would you fill in this sentence for yourself? "God made me _____, and when I _____, I feel His pleasure."

God made each of us unique, and when we act out of that uniqueness, we feel His pleasure. The problem for most of us is that we don't know what makes us unique. We do not experience the joy of knowing God's pleasure *when we run* because we do not know what it is we are supposed to be doing.

The right work energizes us because it is consistent with how we were created and who we were created to be. It is as if we have each been given—as part of our DNA—a proclivity for the right work. The right work fits with our DNA—it fits with who we are and how we were created to reflect our Creator.

One last thought on work. We can even view work as the

primary place where we learn about God. It is easy for us to be godly in the comfortable confines of the church or our small groups of like-minded friends. It is in our work, however, that we put what we theorize about faith into reality. It is in the workplace that our ability to deal with those who do not share our spiritual convictions is tested. In our work, we must face our desire for control, power, and money—just to name a few of the internal struggles we face at work nearly every day.

It is at work where we must deal with the challenge of treating other people (coworkers, customers, clients, etc.) with respect. It is in our work that we struggle with wondering if the claims of Jesus have any bearing on our lives. For most of us, work is an area where we are challenged to put our faith into action. As a result, work becomes a primary laboratory where what we believe is tested against what we do. When we put our faith into action in purposeful and meaningful work, we glorify God and realize the fullness of who He created us to be.

Chapter 5

CHANGING THE PARADIGM
OF RETIREMENT

Remember Michelangelo

O f course if we embrace the idea that work is good and good for us, then we must also reconsider the concept of retirement. It is my contention that retirement—defined as the absence of work—is bad and bad for us.

Since work is essential to our well-being and our worship, the idea of retirement (defined here as the absence of work) is antithetical to our very nature. The idea that we should cease working—cease from what God has created us to do and what is inherently good for us—is in direct opposition to the way God made us. Let's take a deeper look at the concept of retirement.

The first historical record of a society adopting the practice of retirement was in Germany between 1883 and 1889. The German chancellor Otto von Bismarck created model social security laws in an attempt to counter socialist political influences in Germany at that time. In order to solve an unemployment crisis, he came up with the idea of older workers giving up their jobs to open job slots for younger people.

In the United States, President. Franklin Roosevelt instituted

Social Security to solve a similar economic crisis—the Great Depression of the thirties. In Roosevelt's time, the average life expectancy was sixty-three years, so retirement was set at sixty-five. Originally Social Security's minimal financial remuneration wasn't intended to be for everyone; it was intended to offer a financial safety net for those who outlived the average life expectancy. Today the average life expectancy is seventy-six years; if you live to be sixty-five, then your average life expectancy is eighty. If we were to be consistent with the original goals of Social Security, benefits would not be available until a person turns eighty-two.

The first principle concerning work, as discussed in the previous chapter, is that work is good for us. The second principle is that retirement—a relatively new phenomenon—is bad for us. That's right: I said retirement—ceasing to work—is bad for us.

A study done by the Institute of Economic Affairs states that retirement increases your chance of depression by 40 percent and your chance of being diagnosed with a physical condition by 60 percent (www.ieaorg.uk, May 16, 2013). These findings are scary for a culture that has had retirement as its primary objective in life! Additionally research has concluded that retirement can lead to depression, paranoia, schizophrenia, and alcoholism. These disorders apparently arise from (1) shock from job withdrawal, (2) loss of the familiar, (3) loss of job satisfaction, (4) loss of identity, (5) loss of goals, (6) loneliness and a sense of being in the dark, (7) loss of income causing financial instability, and (8) guilt about not working (an effect of the Protestant work ethic). It's not a pretty picture, yet our culture seems obsessed with making retirement our goal. We are even trying to figure out how to retire earlier!

The generation born before the Depression is known as the World War II generation. Those born between 1930 and 1946 are part of the Depression-era generation. Those born between 1946 and 1964 make up the baby boomers.

The World War II generation is mostly gone, leaving its legacy of courage and heroism as a model for future generations. The

Depression-era generation has retired now and is also leaving this world. The baby boomers are retiring and preparing for their life of leisure. But each of these generations has different views of life, work, and retirement.

The World War II generation lived through the Depression, and as such had a clear and personal understanding of financial hardship. Jobs were scarce, and people were desperate. These men and women were glad to have any job they could find. The reality of this hit me when I saw my father's birth certificate. The box titled Occupation listed my grandfather's occupation as unemployed. Those times were tough. Children all over America were born into homes in which the parents weren't sure how they would provide for the next meal. They worked diligently for pennies and were glad to pass on to the next generation a world safe from tyranny and a bright economic future.

For the Depression-era generation, the American Dream meant that they would work hard to acquire a house, family, car, and dog and then retire to a good life of relaxation. While my father and others who were born during the Depression didn't experience the harsh realities of the Dirty Thirties in the way their parents did, they did experience their own harsh childhood realities.

By the time they were entering adulthood, graduating from college, and getting ready to settle down, marry, and begin the dream, the Depression and World War II were over. Opportunities were beginning to flourish, and they wanted more than just a job for survival. My father's generation wanted a good job making more money than their parents and an opportunity to enjoy the good life. These Depression-era babies wanted higher pay, health benefits, a large house in the suburbs, two cars, a college education for their kids, and a retirement plan to provide a comfortable life after they retired. Today this generation has left us and gone to their reward. The baby boomers are retiring to Florida and Arizona, hoping to play golf and die in peace. With today's life expectancy of nearly eighty, these baby boomers who retire at the age of sixty-three may have another seventeen years or more to live. The question remains, "Are they really living?" Retirement for them may not be a blessing; it may prove to be more like a sentence.

Retirement may have been the right idea for a generation whose average life expectancy was sixty-five or seventy years old, but the boomers and the generations behind them need a new paradigm. It is time we took a different look at the concept of retirement. In fact, I'm saying that the time has come to discard the entire concept of retirement. Let's say it: "Never retire!"

PRINCIPLE 3: NEVER RETIRE.

Do you know how old Ronald Reagan was when he became president? He was sixty-nine years old—at least four years past retirement—and he left office when he was seventy-seven years old. Think of the millions of people all over Eastern Europe who are free today because he didn't retire.

I am not saying that the pace of life needs to match the energy level we had in our twenties, and we saw that in Reagan. As we get older, certainly physical realities will slow us all down. Our work may take on a slower pace, but the principle remains the same: we should never cease engaging in some kind of productive, meaningful work. We need to think about what our later years will look like, inclusive of good, productive work that will continue to be an extension of who God made each of us to be.

Remember that for Michelangelo, retirement would have been out of the question; it also should be for us. We need to build a vision for our lives based on the principle that we will never cease being involved in active, productive, meaningful work.

WHAT WORK WILL YOU BE DOING AT EIGHTY-NINE YEARS OLD?

Michelangelo did not stop creating his masterpieces, but he may have slowed down the pace at which he took his chisel to the marble or his brush to the canvas. We need to build a vision for our lives based on a different understanding of what we are going to be doing during the years when we no longer need to work for money.

Chapter 6

INTRODUCTION TO THE PROCESS:

The Journey

If you aim at nothing, you'll hit it every time.
—Zig Ziglar

The *Vision for Your Life* process is similar to planning a trip to Colorado and plotting which mountains you will climb. Imagine you are driving from Eastern Colorado to the Rocky Mountains. Imagine it is that time of night when the stars have just begun to shine, yet there is still enough light to see the mountaintops in the distance. As you drive along Interstate 70 through the flat terrain of Eastern Colorado, you eventually begin to see the Rocky Mountains on the horizon. You can gaze out at that fabulous mountain range and see before you a vast array of choices regarding which mountain to climb.

If you stopped your car and got out to look up at the sky, you could pick a star and make that star your guiding point. It would be your navigational star to determine the direction you would go and which mountains you would climb. *Building a Vision for Your Life* is a process that can be viewed as a journey that has a beginning point (who we are), a navigation point (our personal vision statement), and a definable path along the way (our daily lives). This is similar to the journey we're about to take. We are going to set a star for our lives that serves as a navigational point and define mountains to climb that represent benchmarks in our lives. This process of defining the mountains we'll climb and setting a star for our lives, rooted in who we are, is called *visioneering*, a term I mentioned at the beginning of this book. It means looking at our lives and seeing a picture of what our lives could be about if we're ready to change the basic paradigms we use to shape our future.

But before we can define where we're going, we must know where we're beginning. Before we can find an end point, we must first know our starting point. The starting point for us as human beings is who we are, and the key to understanding who we are— which we will discuss in more detail later—lies in understanding and discovering our deepest motivation. It is that motivation that gets us up in the morning and gives us energy and meaning. I call this our *Core Motivator*. Knowing our *Core Motivator* gives us a starting point—a foundation—from which to plot our vision. When we know our *Core Motivator*, we are able to embrace that which is deepest inside us, the person who we really are, and establish the right starting point for building a vision for our lives.

Chapter 7

CHANGING THE PARADIGM OF WHO YOU ARE:

Your Core Motivator
Know who you are and be it!

I was sitting in a high school gym watching my friend's son Rob play basketball. Rob came down the court unguarded with the ball and with a clear shot at the basket. He hesitated, looked up at his father in the stands, and promptly passed the ball to someone else. When the son saw his father watching him, he became afraid to fail and let someone else take the shot.

My friend was horrified. He stood up in the stands and yelled in frustration, "Know who you are and be it!" You see, my friend knew his son and knew he could make the shot. He did not need to pass off the ball, but he lacked the confidence to take the shot himself. My friend was telling his son to know himself, his gifts, and abilities, and to be that person, no matter who was watching.

Why is it that so few of us—even as adults—know who we are? Why don't we know at our deepest level who we really are, what matters to us most, and what truly, deeply motivates us? Why don't we know the core of the person God created us to be? For each of us, there is a voice inside of us yelling, "Know who you are and be it!"

To begin our journey of *visioneering*, we need the right starting point. We need to start at the beginning to unearth the core of our being and discover—or rediscover—the person God created. Once we have looked inside ourselves to discover who God created us to be, then we are ready to start setting a path for our lives.

Many of us have taken various personality profile tests or done some kind of career assessment. These tests are helpful in describing our personality or our giftedness for a certain career. They do not, however, tell us *who* we are; they only tell us one piece of *what* we are. For example, a personality test might describe you as an extrovert or an introvert. This description is helpful, but it describes what we are, not who we are. Another test might tell us that we have the gifts for accounting, sales, or engineering. Again, this only tells us about what we're good at doing, not who we are.

To help picture this idea, think of an iceberg. On the top, above the waterline, we see our skills, talents, and abilities and the way they are being used in our various life situations. Peeking out from the water's surface is a portion of our personality. It extends from just above the surface to just beneath the surface, and there are parts we would rather hide than have exposed for everyone to see. Beneath our personality is a level of natural gifts, spiritual gifts, and intuition not readily seen but very real and important in understanding who we are. Even further beneath the water's surface is the base of who we are—the person we are at our core. I call this our *Core Motivator*.

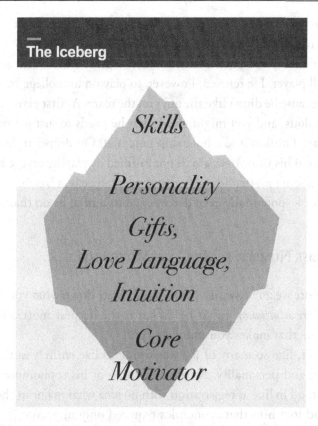

The Iceberg

Skills

Personality

Gifts,
Love Language,
Intuition

Core
Motivator

When we live only out of our skills, personality, or even our gifts, we are dissatisfied because the deepest needs in our lives are not being met.

Think of eating French food. The best part of French food is always the sauce—that rich, creamy sauce filled with enough calories to give everyone except the French (who have the lowest rate of heart disease in the world), a heart attack. If we only eat the sauce, we will starve to death. We need the meat of the dish—the *Core Motivator*—for the necessary nutrition to keep us healthy and energized. The sauce, like our skills, personality, and gifts, is important and tastes great, but without the meat, the sauce is worthless.

Let me be clear here because this is important. When we live out of our gifts, personality, or skills as the primary source of our being

35

and starve the true core of who we are, then we will feel emotionally malnourished and unfulfilled in our lives.

For example, I have a friend who is a great athlete and a great baseball player. He refused, however, to play on his college baseball team because he didn't like the guys on the team. At first glance, that is ridiculous, and you might think that he needs to just get over it and play. Think of the scholarship potential. On deeper reflection, however, if his *Core Motivator* is not fulfilled by playing on the team, then it doesn't matter how gifted and talented he is at baseball—it is worthless—potentially even detrimental to him to be on that team.

EXERCISE NUMBER 1: MY CORE MOTIVATOR IS …

Before we go forward, I want you to write down what you think your *Core Motivator* might be. What is the deepest motivation at your core that makes you uniquely you?

Scott, like so many of us, was trying to live entirely out of his skill set and personality. At the beginning of his sophomore year, Scott stood in line at registration with no idea what major to choose. A friend told him that economics required only nine core courses, and he could take the rest of his degree in electives. Scott did a little research and found out that economics required some math (but not too much) and some conceptual thinking. Scott was good at both and felt his skills were a good match for this major.

Scott had no idea what he wanted to do with his life, but the job prospects for economics majors seemed pretty good (banking, finance, etc.), so he became an economics major. He graduated from college, got a job with a bank, and developed his skills, personality, and gifts around his job.

After a successful career in the financial field, he lives with the gnawing uncertainty that there might be something better for him. He wonders if this is all there is to life. He is only forty years old; he has a great job, a wonderful wife, and three beautiful kids, but there is something tragically missing. He has lost his passion and his drive. He looks at his father and realizes that his father worked hard all his life to retire well-off, but somehow the thought of grinding out an existence for the next twenty-five years in order to retire just doesn't seem to make sense to him. Depression is knocking on the door, and Scott needs to take some big steps to avoid it.

How did Scott get here? How did a simple decision to become an economics major determine other decisions that ended up with him sitting behind a nice desk staring at spreadsheets? How did living and working out of his skill set and personality drive him to a life of emptiness and a lack of fulfillment?

The most terrifying questions of all lurk just beneath the surface: Is he doomed to a passionless existence for the rest of his life? Did Scott make a huge mistake by choosing economics as a major or taking a job in the financial field?

The problem might not be his major in college or his career. Maybe Scott is in exactly the right position for who he is. Perhaps he is in the perfect job, and the question for him is how to do his job out of the context of who he is. In other words, perhaps he needs to do the same job but out of the context of his true *Core Motivator*. Maybe he needs to do his job and live the rest of his life out of the meat, not the sauce. Maybe he is living out of his skills, personality, and gifts instead of living out of his *Core Motivator*.

The question will remain for Scott and us:

How do we know that the life we are currently living is the right path for us?

The key to understanding who we are and if we're living out of the meat or the sauce lies in discovering our *Core Motivator*. In the next section, we are going to (1) define the term *Core Motivator* and (2) understand the importance of knowing our *Core Motivator* in forming a vision for our lives. Then we can move into chapters nine and ten and discuss the exercises needed to help us discover our *Core Motivator*.

In order to understand our *Core Motivator*, we must define the term.

DEFINING CORE MOTIVATOR

Your Core Motivator is that which drives you and through which you take every action. It is why you do what you do the way you do it.

We moved to Canada in February 1996. No one should move to Canada in February, but we did. One of the first assignments in my new position was to lead a visioning time for our management team. I was given an article from the *Harvard Business Review,* titled, "Building Your Company's Vision," a summary of the book *Built to Last* by Jim Collins and Jerry Porras.[1] The Harvard article highlighted Collins and Porras's concept of core values for organizations and the idea that we must begin our visioning by identifying those core values. I was struck by their idea and began to think that this concept of looking at core principles could be applied to people as well as organizations.

My concern has always been for people more than organizations, and perhaps my twenty years of working with students in the nonprofit world has shaped the way I think. As I thought about the article, I realized that we are all unique people and that each of us seems to have a view of life that comes from deep inside of us. I saw this many times in the students I worked with, and Collins and Porras's work gave me a framework to think about how we each uniquely view the world.

What immediately struck me was the idea that while we might be looking for core values in an organization, in people we are looking for a *Core Motivator*. A *Core Motivator* is different from core values because values are shaped by external forces. They are developed as part of the life of the organization, and they can change over time. In fact, the core values of an organization are often the result of the *Core Motivator* of a person or people leading that organization, but I will reserve that discussion for later in the book. An individual's *Core Motivator* is hard-wired from birth and will never change. It is part of their DNA and is God's handiwork in their creation.

When thinking of a visioning process for individuals, we must begin by identifying a person's *Core Motivator.*

It is important for us to know our Core Motivator because it

1. *is a reflection of the nature of God in us,*
2. *gives us a unique competitive advantage,*
3. *brings continuity into our lives,*
4. *avoids the dangers of not knowing who we are, and*
5. *is what energizes us.*

A REFLECTION OF GOD'S NATURE IN US

As I processed this idea of *Core Motivator,* a convergence of several factors in my life occurred. I looked back on my years of working with people and reflected also on the theology of creation I had learned in seminary. I realized that our *Core Motivator* is a reflection of the very nature of God in us. We have been created in the image of God and are therefore image bearers of God's nature— we reflect His very nature. When we think of our *Core Motivator,* we are thinking of that part of God's nature that is hardwired in us, His created being, and in our DNA. We see ourselves as part of God's work in creation.

It is true that sometimes it is difficult to see the hand of God in His creation. When we see natural disasters, starving children, wars, crime, murder, and abuse, it can be hard to tell that God is in charge. At the same time, when we see the Alps or the Rocky Mountains or a newborn baby or one friend forgiving another, it is hard not to see the hand of God.

This parallel exists for each of our individual lives as well. When we look honestly at our own lives and see our personal flaws and failures, it is difficult to see the image of God in us. It is only when we look beyond our flaws and failures to see our *Core Motivator* that we can see the handiwork of God in our lives. As we look deeply at ourselves and understand our *Core Motivator*, we see not only our failings but also the marvelous hand of God, who created us beautifully and uniquely. By looking at what is deepest in us—our *Core Motivator*—we see a glimpse of God, and we can marvel that we have been created in His image. We are image bearers, and we reflect His nature and glory in our being. God created us in His image, and His image is to be found in the deepest part of who we are—our *Core Motivator*.

Our Deepest Motivation

In addition to seeing God's workmanship in our lives by seeing our *Core Motivator*, we can also see that our *Core Motivator* is what drives us to choose the various activities we engage in. Because our *Core Motivator* is part of our hardwiring from creation, we learn to do whatever it takes to satisfy it. Conversely when our *Core Motivator* is not satisfied, we are dissatisfied with our lives, no matter how good the other factors surrounding our lives may be.

In other words, if we have all the material comforts this world may offer, but our *Core Motivator* remains unfulfilled, we will not be satisfied because the very essence of our nature from creation is being starved. We, like Scott, can be miserable inside our perfect lives. While we have all the trimmings of a great life, what is deepest inside of us is starving. We are therefore in a constant state of groping for those activities that we think will most satisfy our *Core Motivator*.

This becomes incredibly problematic when we don't know our *Core Motivator.*

Chas was a successful banker who had built his career on his skills learned through years in the industry, his sharp intellect, and his winsome personality. But Chas spent much of his time either alone in his office or at large social gatherings representing the bank. His deep frustration came from not having his *Core Motivator* satisfied. He is a *Connecting Core Motivator* and as such needed one-on-one relationships to satisfy his deepest core.

Eventually Chas was promoted and became responsible for a group of five other bankers. Jim was one of the people who reported to Chas, and he dropped into Chas's office every day just to talk and catch up with him. Jim was a good banker but not particularly better than the other four members of the team. The others in the group generally stayed to themselves, making loans and developing their portfolios. Chas, however, believed that Jim was the most outstanding banker in the group, and he praised him and rewarded him above the others. He didn't see that although the production of all five of the people who reported to him was essentially identical, he valued Jim above the others because Jim connected with him relationally. The very act of Jim coming into Chas's office every day and talking to him made Chas value Jim over the others. Why? It's because Jim has the same *Core Motivator* as Chas. Jim was meeting Chas's need to have his *Core Motivator* satisfied, and Chas didn't even know it.

We tend to hold those with the same *Core Motivator* in higher esteem than those with different *Core Motivators.* Without even knowing it, we validate what we see in others when it connects with what is deepest in ourselves.

CORE MOTIVATOR: YOUR UNIQUE COMPETITIVE ADVANTAGE

Your *Core Motivator* makes you unique, and uniqueness pays off in all kinds of areas. In my twenty-two years of working with high school kids, I understood the powerful influence of peer pressure on that age group. I was also keenly aware that the truly remarkable kids—the ones that lead the pack—are the ones who are unique in their confidence and secure in who they are. They stand out from the crowd because they know that what makes them different is also what makes them great.

We each have a unique, God-given design with great fundamental qualities. It is our uniqueness that makes us great, and our *Core Motivator* is the heart of that uniqueness.

One day I heard an interview with a record producer being asked what he was looking for in young talent. The guy said, "People will say to me, 'I sound just like Stevie Wonder' or some other big star.'" My response is "We already have Stevie Wonder, and we don't need another one. We are looking for someone with a unique sound."

Our challenge is to understand and live out of our *Core Motivator* and by so doing, allow our own unique sound to differentiate us from the many other people to whom we are similar.

Your unique competitive advantage stems from how you do things in a way that is uniquely you. As an individual, the most sustainable and effective way to create this unique twist—to have your own sound—is to live out of your *Core Motivator*.

BRINGING CONTINUITY TO OUR LIVES BY UNDERSTANDING OUR CORE MOTIVATORS

I attended the Charles Hobbs Time Management (producers of the Day-Timer system of time management) seminar many years ago. At one point, the session was opened for questions. A young professional raised his hand and asked, "I have one Day-Timer for my personal life and one Day-Timer for my business life. Is that OK?"

With the seriousness of a graveside preacher, the seminar instructor held up her Day-Timer and said, "One life, one Day-Timer." In other words, the twenty-four hours in each day belong to one person, and what you do in your work is not segmented from what you do in your personal life. We live one life, and we must manage that life—both our work and our leisure—as one entity.

The first step in bringing continuity to our lives is to define our *Core Motivator*. Only when we know who we are at our deepest level can we then build a picture for our lives that includes every aspect of our lives in a congruent way.

THE CONSEQUENCES OF NOT KNOWING YOUR CORE MOTIVATOR

When we do not know our *Core Motivator*, it is impossible to live proactively out of the core of who we are. We cannot leverage the best and most unique part of our creation—our strongest suit—because we don't know what that strong suit is. Over a period of time, as we continue to search for who we are, we develop a persona that may not reflect our true person.

Ned had been made fun of in elementary school because of a slight physical defect. Ned was the class clown and the butt of many jokes. He developed a persona that was an extreme people pleaser. By the time he was thirty years old, he was convinced that this was his true person. Yet something deep inside of him knew there was more to life than being an underemployed, grown-up child. He wanted to be his true self but fought hard to hold on to the character he had created and had become so comfortable playing. He had to kill the character in order to give new life to the true person.

As I have consulted with many people, helping them discover their *Core Motivators*, I have noticed a common thread. Most of us, like Ned, have developed a second persona—a character who is a false self. As I speak with individuals, I find that the person they initially tell me they are not who they really are. They have created—usually at an early age—another character that they play on the world's stage, a character they come to see as their true identity, but it's not.

Often, we hide behind this character so that no one will see the true person we are. We believe the character is more acceptable to the rest of the world than our true selves. Most of the time, this character is developed in the formative years as a response to overwhelming peer pressure.

As time goes on, and we grow up, we become so accustomed to playing this role that we lose touch with who we really are. We come to know this character better than we know our true selves. We have played the role for so long that we find it doubly difficult to know who we are and be it. We have been lost in the other persona, and we don't know who we are.

I will talk more about this in chapter 11, but for now, we need to understand that this problem becomes a double-edged sword. On one edge, we don't know ourselves since we don't know our *Core Motivator*, and on the opposite edge, we are pretending to be someone we are not.

Our Core Motivator Is What Energizes Us

We are most energized in life by living out who we are at our core. When we are living out of our *Core Motivator*, we approach our life and work with a feeling of confidence and excitement that cannot be replicated by living out of our gifts and skills. We get up in the morning ready to do that which we were created to do. We have a deep sense of joy in living out of our deepest motivation, and we have great peace in knowing that we are being the person God created us to be. We bring all of who we are to our relationships, and we engage the world around us with a new sense of genuineness and congruency. Understanding our *Core Motivator* can be life-changing because it enables us—perhaps for the first time—to be truly free to be the person God created us to be.

Chapter 8

CORE MOTIVATOR—THE SECRET SAUCE

There are very few genuinely new ideas in this world, yet the *Core Motivator* is a powerful new idea. Your *Core Motivator* determines why you do what you do, and the way you do it. It is the lens through which you see all of life. It is who you are, and that is a new idea.

THE SEVEN CORE MOTIVATORS

Why does one person spend all day fixing his friend's fence? Why does another person move from job to job every two or three years out of boredom? Why does someone else endure one painful relationship after another? Why does another person obsess over details? Why does someone else always want to please people? Why do some people need a best friend?

Each of these individuals has a different *Core Motivator*, and their outward actions tell us about who these people are on the inside and how they view life. Their actions reflect their talents, gifts, and personalities, but more importantly, they reflect the person's *Core Motivator*.

As I've said earlier, each one of us has a distinct *Core Motivator* through which he or she performs these actions.

When I began working with people to help them discover their *Core Motivators*, I did not really know what we were looking for. All I knew was that we were looking for something that was the core of who they were and a reflection of the nature of God.

Each *Core Motivator* had to be a reflection of the nature of God in us, so I was looking for that thing that was in each person that was also in the nature of God. I would ask each client what they thought their *Core Motivator* was, and often, I would get responses like *success, competition, money, sex,* or something similar, but none of those things were part of the very nature of God so I knew they were not *Core Motivators*. God, for example, is not competitive or concerned with success. He doesn't need money or approval, and these are not part of His very nature.

After about one hundred clients, I began to see the same seven *Core Motivators* repeat and I developed the following list.

The seven Core Motivators are

1. *Connecting,*
2. *Belonging,*
3. *Caring,*
4. *Serving,*
5. *Giving,*
6. *Creating, and*
7. *Perfecting.*

After I had identified the seven *Core Motivators*, I saw them as fitting into three groups as follows:

1. *People for people's sake.* The first two *Core Motivators*, *Connecting* and *Belonging*, are *people Core Motivators*. That is, they focus on people for people's sake. They do not require a task in order to be operative.

2. *Task for task's sake.:* The last two *Core Motivators, Creating* and *Perfecting,* are *task Core Motivators.* They are task-oriented and do not need people in order to function.

3. *Tasks directed at people.* The middle three *Core Motivators, Caring, Serving,* and *Giving,* are tasks directed at people. That is, they are primarily task-oriented but require a person to be the object of the task in order to be exercised. (You can't serve a chair—you have to have a person to serve.)

DEFINING THE CORE MOTIVATORS

1. *Connecting*—God is a relational God who desires to connect with His people. This *Core Motivator* is focused on one-on-one relationships. People with this *Core Motivator* are energized by the individual connection or *chemistry* they have with another person. They do not need a task to accomplish in order to be energized; they simply need engagement with another person.

   Example:

   Jack has built his practice by meeting with clients one-on-one and has developed a large, client-based business. He is energized by the individual meetings and feels like his day is best when he has a series of these kinds of meetings all day. At a party, he will seek out one person to talk to, and when he is finished having an individual conversation, or conversations, with the people he wants to talk to, he is ready to go home. He feels alone in groups, and if there is no one in the group with whom he connects, then he will leave that group. The worst thing he can do is sit alone in front of his computer.

2. *Belonging*—God is a belonging God; He is three in one—Father, Son, and Holy Spirit. This *Core Motivator* is focused on groups or teams. People with this *Core Motivator* are

energized by belonging to a team or group of people and do not necessarily need connection with the various individuals on the team. They just need the team. They also do not need a task to accomplish; they are energized by simply being with the team. They are not particularly energized by one-on-one engagements and in fact, can find them quite draining. They too are de-energized by sitting alone in front of their computer.

Example:

Corey loves the team. It doesn't matter to him what the team is doing. He just loves being on the team. His best memories are of playing football in high school, and he feels he was most energized in life when he was a part of that team. He builds his business by gathering a team of people around him and feels that the best part of his day or week is his team meeting. When given a task, he thinks, *Who else can do this with me?*

3. *Caring*—God is a caring God who sees all of our needs and cares for us. This *Core Motivator* is focused on the task of providing help for someone in need. *Caring Core Motivators* are drawn to needy people. Meeting the emotional, spiritual, or physical needs of another person energizes people with this *Core Motivator*. They sometimes struggle to find connections with healthy people and even find it difficult to sustain relationships with people who were once needy and then move to a state of health.

Example:

Mark is drawn to needy people. He loves to come alongside a hurting person and take care of him or her. Engaging with a needy person regardless of whether that person ever gets any better energizes him. Mark is also a leader, and often those whom he has helped will follow him out of gratitude for his concern. Mark is therefore able to build his business based on how he cares for his staff and customers. When I took a tour of Mark's business, I noticed that every person I met had one need or another. One person had just had major surgery, one was handicapped, and one was just out of an abusive relationship. I knew immediately Mark was a *Caring Core Motivator*.

4. *Serving*—God is a serving God and Jesus was the servant king. This *Core Motivator* is focused on the task of providing service to someone or some group. Unlike the *Caring Core Motivator*, this person is drawn to people's needs rather than needy people. That nuance is significant in understanding the difference between the two *Core Motivators*. For a person with this *Core Motivator*, performing tasks that help others energizes him.

   Example:

   One of my sons is a *Serving Core Motivator*. When we were moving from Canada, we were having the carpet replaced in our house and the workman told me I would lose my office for a day while he installed the new carpet, which was OK with me. At the end of the second day without my office, I was not a happy camper. I was stepping over the guy in disgust annoyed that he was taking so long. My *Serving Core Motivator* son walked in from school, took one look at the guy, and said, "Can I offer you a glass of water or something?" The guy looked up and said, "Yea, that would be great." My son saw what I did not—a guy with a need—and was thrilled to meet that need.

5. *Giving*—God is a giving God, who gave His only Son for us. This *Core Motivator* is focused on the task of meeting a specific need by providing a specific benefit—often but not exclusively monetary. People with this *Core Motivator* are energized by the act of giving, either of their money, their talents, or themselves.

   Example:

   Kurt has a hard time not giving. He will randomly hand a check to someone he believes deserves it because he loves to give. He sees his engagements with other people as an opportunity to give up his time, wisdom, or money. After Kurt had been a client, he landed a big job running a major division of a bank. As a follow-up, I asked him to meet me for breakfast so I could pitch some additional services working with his new team. At the end of breakfast, he handed me a check. I said, "What is this for?" He said, "I know your time is valuable, and I just wanted to give you this for meeting with me."

I told him, "This is quintessential for a *Giving Core Motivator*. I'll take your check. You just bought yourself some coaching."

6. *Creating*—God is a creating God who created all things for His glory. This *Core Motivator* is focused on the task of developing something new. Diagnosing the problem and creating a solution energizes the person with *Creating* as their *Core Motivator*.

Example:

Brad sees every house on the block as something he could make better, and every empty lot a place where he could build something. He buys a house for the purpose of improving on it, and when he has finished the various projects, he is ready to move again. This is his approach to all of life. He gets bored when there is nothing new to create and will create opportunities where one does not exist.

7. *Perfecting*—God is perfect and holy. This *Core Motivator* is focused on the task of making what already exists perfect. People with this *Core Motivator* are energized by taking steps to make something perfect and seeing it come to fruition.

Example:

Ted sees what perfection looks like in all of life. In every situation, he sees how it could be perfect and is frustrated by the flaws in life. He spends a lot of time on a single task in an attempt to make it perfect. If he cannot see a way to make something perfect, he will be paralyzed in completing the task.

THE SINFUL/NEGATIVE MANIFESTATION

With each *Core Motivator*, there is a negative—or what the Bible calls a sinful—manifestation. While it is true that God created each of us in His image, it is also true that each of us is affected by the fall of creation into sin. The perfect state that God created has been corrupted by the fall, and no element of creation has escaped that corruption. Therefore, our *Core Motivator* has not only the means to glorify God but also its negative, corrupted side of dishonoring God as well. All sin is rooted in the same place as that of Adam and Eve. When Satan tempted them, he told them they would be like God, and that desire to take the place of God was the root of their sin—and ours. When we see the sinful manifestation of our *Core Motivator*, we also see our desire to be like God and to replace what belongs to God with our own ability. Below is the list of *Core Motivators* with their corresponding most common negative attributes.

1. *Connecting*—high regard for what other people think of them. The worst thing for them is to be rejected by another person. This can result in their rejecting other people quickly before they can be rejected. They sometimes hurt others before others can hurt them. They fall into sin by believing that the approval and love of other people can replace the love of God.

2. *Belonging*—high need to please everyone in a group. Because this can result in an inability to make decisions without complete consensus, they can be *wafflers* and can be seen as disingenuous; they tell each person in a group what they think that person wants to hear. They fall into sin by

believing that belonging to a human team can take the place of belonging to God.

3. *Caring*—high need to take care of people, resulting in arrogance. They can cross the line between caring for people and taking care of them. While it is great to care for people, it becomes arrogant to say, essentially, "I know what's best for you, and I will take care of you." They fall into sin by believing that God cannot take care of someone, but they can.

4. *Serving*—daily struggle with pride based on the tasks they have accomplished in helping someone with a need. They struggle with a desire for other people to recognize them for what they have done. They are proud of their service but also very sensitive to being used by people; they can be suspicious of people taking advantage of them. Sometimes they use people in order to keep the relationship in balance or in their view to keep the score even. They have an equation in their head that goes something like "If I use you, then I will feel OK about serving you." They fall into sin by believing that God will not serve someone, but they will.

5. *Giving*—a strong tendency toward becoming haughty. They see themselves as having more to give than others and can develop an attitude of smug superiority. They fall into sin by believing that God has withheld blessing from a person, but they can provide what the person needs.

6. *Creating*—highly likely to become critical and judgmental. They see what can be created, but they also see what is wrong and how it can be fixed. They fall into sin by believing that God has not done a very good job creating, but they can do better.

7. *Perfecting*—the tendency to develop perfectionism. They see how all of life could be perfect and have a difficult time accepting anything that is not perfect. They are often paralyzed because they cannot begin a task they cannot

complete perfectly. They fall into sin by believing that God did not make things perfect, but they can.

Exercise Number 2: Identify Your Core Motivator

In the next chapter, we'll discover how to identify your *Core Motivator*. However, before we do that, take a good look at the seven *Core Motivators* and ask yourself two questions. One, which *Core Motivator* do I think I am? Two, which *Core Motivator* do I not want to be?

Chapter 9

DISCOVERING YOUR CORE MOTIVATOR

Discovering your *Core Motivator* can be painful, and it takes courage. Discovering your *Core Motivator* causes you to look inside yourself at both the good and the bad, and sometimes it is painful to face the bad inside of you. In fact, typically we will first see the *Core Motivator* in its negative or sinful manifestation. This means that you may be able to look at your fears, the ugly things you do, and the bad ways in which you treat people and see behind them your *Core Motivator*.

In fact, you may find that while you have been trying to hide your *Core Motivator* for many years, you now must face the person you've always been deep inside. That prospect will be frightening for many of us and will put us at a point of great vulnerability and fear.

Yet as you face who you are and confront your ugly side, the potential exists for a kind of freedom you have never before experienced. You can finally be free to enjoy who God made you to be and rejoice in being that entire person. You can live the character-driven life you were created to live. You can give your gifts and abilities to others in a new and fulfilling way.

Ralph

Hired by a printing firm to do some vision consulting for two partners, I began by interviewing each partner separately. My initial interview with Ralph went well enough. Although we had a discussion that stayed on the surface, it was what I had expected. In our next meeting, we began to talk about more important issues in Ralph's life. As we talked and I learned more about him, I asked him a question that was obviously too close to a sensitive area for him. He would not answer the question, and that was the last time we talked. He bowed out of the process because he couldn't handle my asking those kinds of deep questions. He didn't want anyone (including himself, perhaps) to see beyond the surface to the deepest parts of his life.

Few of us can handle such questions and such exposure. We have spent a lot of time (most of our lives) and energy (we are exhausted), keeping the painful parts of our lives from being exposed. The wall we have built to keep others out is the same wall that keeps us trapped. We have become prisoners in our own play. We are locked into plot-driven lives because we are afraid of the character that might be revealed if we let anyone see who we really are.

We must have the courage to face our own reality—to look at our lives in their entirety and embrace the totality of who we are. We must face the negative manifestations of who we are, and we must look deep inside ourselves in order to discover the unique and wonderful person whom God created us to be.

Ben

Ben approached me after I had spoken at a seminar on *Vision for Your Life* and asked if he could talk to me about some issues he was having. Since I had only about thirty minutes before another session began, I invited him to walk with me to the next venue. Ben said he had recently been let go from his second people-oriented job in two years. He was devastated and didn't understand what had happened to him. He had worked hard to get to the top of an organization and had been made president. Then when he should have been flying high, the board unceremoniously fired him. He blamed the board for its pettiness and shortsightedness. He quickly found a job as president of another organization. Within a year, the board of that organization also fired him.

Ben told me that he was certain his *Core Motivator* was *Connecting*. When I asked him to describe the picture of his life if money were no object, he painted a picture of himself sitting in an office writing a manual of some kind. When I pointed out to him that there were no people in that picture, he began to reconsider his initial thought that *Connecting* was his *Core Motivator*. In fact, Ben's *Core Motivator* has nothing to do with people, yet he spent most of his life aspiring to positions leading people. He had created a persona of being a people person, but it wasn't the real him. In fact, he had created that persona so well that he was able to get two boards of directors to hire him into high-profile, people-oriented jobs. But once in those jobs, the real person could not match the persona, and he was fired.

The next step for Ben was to look at his life and discover why he had aspired to lead people even though his *Core Motivator* had nothing to do with people. He was going to have to face his sin.

As we talked, he told me that as a young boy, the popular, athletic kids in school had never accepted him. When he became president of those two organizations, he viewed the board members the same way he had seen those popular kids in fifth grade, and he hated them. In a short time, his distaste for the board members became clear, and they let him go.

Ben was talking about things that had been buried deep inside of him for many years, and they all came out in a twenty-minute conversation. As he searched for his *Core Motivator*, he faced those painful memories and also faced his own sin. Ben's sin was not simply that he hated the popular kids but something deeper; he wanted to be someone other than the person God had created him to be. He wanted to be accepted by people more than he wanted to be accepted by God, and this sin caused great pain for him, his family, and many others.

Exercise Number 3: Write Your Life History

It is time for you to undertake another important exercise. I want you to stop reading this book and write out your life history in less than twenty pages. There are no other instructions. Just write it out. Once you have finished writing, you may return to the rest of this chapter.

Stop reading now.

Embrace Your Weakness

Sam

As he sat across the desk, Sam appeared to be very frustrated with me. He had asked me to do some consulting for him, so we were working through developing a vision for his life by talking about his personal biography.

He said, "Bob, the reason I hired you was because I thought you would bring a spiritual perspective to this process. We haven't talked at all about God."

I said, "Sam, you've got to trust me. We're going to talk about God, but when we do, we're going to move beyond the simple religious clichés you think I should be saying."

We talked more about who Sam was and who he had become. As we looked at Sam's life, he had to face his sin. Finally in frustration, he said, "Bob, do you want to know the truth? I use people. I am only friends with people from whom I can get something. I am friends with you because I get something from your teaching. If I ever stop learning from you, I'll stop being friends with you." For Sam, this was not a threat; it was simply a recognition of who he was and how he acted. He knew himself well enough to know that what he had just realized about himself was absolutely true. He was embarrassed and horrified, but he was facing his sin.

I admit I was a little surprised. Sam is a great guy who always seemed available to help others. By recognizing himself as a user of other people, Sam was now getting close to his *Core Motivator*. He was facing his sin.

It is painful for all of us to face our sin (that which we know is wrong). We have shoved our sin deep down into our subconscious, where we think we can escape it. It is painful but necessary to come to grips with our sins because only then can we honestly look at who we really are. Only when we are brutally honest with all of who we are can we finally identify that which is central to our very being.

In fact, we can sometimes see our *Core Motivator* most clearly in its sinful manifestation.

As Sam and I talked some more, he told me how as a child he was always doing things for his friends. Eventually he felt he was being used, and he was ashamed and hurt. He was ashamed that he could be so easily used by others. As a result, he saw himself as weak instead of the tough guy he wanted to be.

Sam had decided that the best defense was a good offense, and he learned to use others before they could use him. In this way, he felt that as long as the score was even—he used others, and they used him—he was in control of the situation. Sam had developed a user's paradigm. It was the sinful manifestation of his uniquely God-created *Core Motivator*.

Sam never felt the freedom to really be who God had created him to be. Sam's *Core Motivator* was *Serving*, but instead of seeing *Serving* as his strength, he saw it as his weakness.

Sam is happiest when he is living out of his *Core Motivator* when he is being the person God created him to be—a person who serves. Sam also is quite gifted in his chosen profession. He is great at what he does, has won international recognition, and likes his craft. The goal for Sam was not to change what he did for a living, instead change the way he approached his craft. Instead of looking for ways to use clients, he would look for ways to serve them.

Together we developed a new business plan for him that was built on a model of providing high-end service to fewer customers (at higher rates), instead of trying to churn through a lot of customers at lower rates and a lower level of service. In other words, we changed the paradigm from using customers to serving them and getting compensated for his high level of service.

Most of us think our *Core Motivator* is our greatest weakness. We have convinced ourselves that what motivates us most deeply is a weakness. We believe that we must work our entire lives to overcome this perceived weakness.

It is worth noting here that I haven't said it *is* our weakness, only that we perceive it as our weakness. In reality, what we believe to be our greatest weakness is actually our greatest strength. It's a paradox of life that our *Core Motivator*—our strongest suit—somehow strikes us as our greatest weakness.

Before you begin to analyze your life history, take a look back at the *Core Motivator* list in the previous chapter. Look at the seven *Core Motivators* and ask, "Which one feels weakest?" or "Which one do I *not* want it to be?" There is a good chance that your answer is your *Core Motivator*.

THREE WAYS TO DETERMINE YOUR CORE MOTIVATOR

There are three basic ways to identify your *Core Motivator*. The first and most common way is to look for themes in your life. The second way is to look for glaring negative or sinful manifestations. The third way is to look for change points. In each case, the best method for beginning is to write out your life history. Perhaps you've been putting it off and have read up to this point without completing the assignment. If so, I encourage you to begin now. Come back to chapter 10 once your life story is written down.

Chapter 10

YOUR LIFE HISTORY ANALYSIS

After you have completed your personal biography, it is time for some self-analysis. You are going to need to be brutally honest with yourself as you survey your personal biography.

PERFECTING

The first thing to look for in your personal life history is an inability to actually write it. If you couldn't write your life history (or wrote less than two pages), then your *Core Motivator* may be *Perfecting*. *Perfecting Core Motivators* struggle mightily with this exercise. Since they cannot write their own story perfectly, they are paralyzed and can't write it at all.

I remember one client who was scheduled to meet with me but kept putting off sending me his life story. The day before we were to meet, he called and said that he would have to cancel our meeting because he had not completed the assignment. I encouraged him to come anyway, which he did. I had a pretty good idea his *Core Motivator* was *Perfecting* because *Perfecting Core Motivators* usually find it impossible to write their life history. I told him to simply sit at my computer and type out the basic outline—a task I thought would take him about an hour.

Three hours later, he appeared with his history and said that he couldn't believe how helpful this exercise had been. His *Core Motivator* was indeed *Perfecting*, and once he was given the freedom to just sit down and write it, he was able to let the memories flow. It was the fear of not doing it perfectly that had paralyzed him prior to our meeting.

I have seen this pattern over and over with *Perfecting Core Motivators*. When I am working in a corporate setting and clients are required by their boss to submit a life history to me, I will sometimes get a very basic page of bullet points or something similar. These people know they have to write something because their boss has commanded them to complete the exercise, but it is painful for them. They put it off as long as they can, and at the last minute, they write out as little as possible—bullet points on one page. When this occurs, it is a clue that we are probably looking at a *Perfecting Core Motivator*.

Another clue for *Perfecting Core Motivators* is the walls in their office. The classic *Perfecting Core Motivator* has nothing on his or her walls because they can't decide what the perfect thing would be to put on the walls.

I have also observed that they tend to be habitually late because they cannot leave the last thing until they feel it is perfect.

These are just some of the clues to a *Perfecting Core Motivator*, but they are some of the traits that I have seen repeated with this *Core Motivator*.

Perfecting Core Motivators see the world through the lens of how it could be perfect. They see the daily tasks they must accomplish as needing to be perfect and the people and tasks that are not perfect frustrate them. If they can't do something perfectly, then they don't want to do it at all.

Of course, nothing in life is perfect, and *Perfecting Core Motivators* can have a very difficult time. They tend to be very hard on themselves and those whom they care about, as well as their coworkers. They see how others could be perfect and don't understand why they are not striving for the same goal of perfection as they are.

Additionally, they have been told their entire lives to change the way they look at the world. They have been called perfectionists and have been told to let go of it. I believe the *Perfecting Core Motivator* is the most difficult of all the *Core Motivators* to navigate because of the tremendous frustration of living in an imperfect world. Nonetheless, I know some very successful and vision-filled *Perfecting Core Motivators*.

The key for them is to understand the value they bring to the team. One of my *Perfecting Core Motivator* clients is a bank president, and when the banking crisis happened in 2008, it was critical that he command the ship when the regulators came to inspect the bank. The books were perfect, and the bank survived.

He fights perfectionism every day, but he also embraces the *Perfecting* every day—and that is the key. *Perfecting Core Motivators* need to embrace their perfecting while struggling against *perfectionism*. Perfectionism is a frustrating and depressing beat-your-head-against-the-wall exercise. Nothing will ever be perfect. *Perfecting*, however, is a needed and essential part of the body of Christ because we need some members of the body to show us what perfect would look like.

One of my best friends is a *Perfecting Core Motivator*. He would always point out the errors in my newsletters, and it was quite annoying. Eventually I asked him if I could send them to him first and have him edit them before I sent them to my mailing list, and he agreed. His *Perfecting* is helping me have better newsletters!

Do you struggle with perfectionism? Do you have high stress when things are not done perfectly? Were you unable to write your life history? Are the walls in your office or home barren? Are you constantly late for things? If the answer to these questions is yes, then you might be a *Perfecting Core Motivator*.

The Other Core Motivators

If you did write your life history, let's look at (1) the positive themes, (2) the negative or sinful manifestations, and (3) the potential change points.

We'll begin by looking at change points. When speaking of change points, we're looking for a dramatic event in your life after which everything changed. Are there points in time you can point to and say, "I changed after that" or "I changed because of that"?

Chad

Chad went through *Vision for Your Life* as part of a corporate group exercise. When I first read his life history, it was very difficult to detect either a theme or any negative manifestations. We delved more into his life and focused on what turned out to be a major change point.

When Chad was in eighth grade, he was in a coma. During this time, he was aware of everything that was happening around him. He was aware of all the people who came to visit— including his friends and what they were saying about him. He remembers resolving to change everything about who he was if he ever returned to a normal life. When Chad awakened from the coma, he changed everything about who he was.

When I met Chad, he was thirty-two years old and had no idea of who he really was; he only knew the person he had become after the coma. From sketchy evidence of his life before the coma, we guessed that his *Core Motivator* might be *Belonging*. I asked him to live with that for a couple of weeks to see if it felt right to him. He came back in a couple of weeks and said that yes, it was right, and he was finally free to be the person he was created to be.

Or take Jake. Jake was walking home from school in fifth grade and was beaten up by some other kids who preyed on his weakness. He vowed to never be taken advantage of again and changed everything about himself. He made himself into someone he was not, and by the time he was thirty years old, he didn't know who he was. When we went back to that change point, we were able to recover the kid whose weakness was actually his greatest strength.

At the very least, this process of looking back at our lives gives us some insight into who we were before or after the change points. Looking at these points of change, we can see places where we either became less of who we are or in some cases, more of who we are. In either case, the goal is to focus on who we are—in the sense of who God made us to be. The goal is to discover the person God created us to be, apart from the person we have conformed ourselves into being. Very few people have these kinds of dramatic change points, but if you do, then it is worth trying to recall who you were before the change point.

THEMES

Remember if you were unable to write your life history or if it only took up a page or two, you are probably a *Perfecting Core Motivator*. Now let's look at the other six *Core Motivators* and see what kind of themes would be present for each.

By *themes,* I mean the main points or highlights in what you have chosen to write about. In other words, when you look at your life, how do you see it? What themes emerge as you think about your life? Remember that your *Core Motivator* is the lens through which you see all of life, so look at what you've written and see what lens you were using. Take a look back at your life timeline. Look for the highlights and themes.

CONNECTING

Connecting Core Motivators typically see life through the lens of the various people with whom they've had deep relationships. Their life histories look something like "When I was in fourth grade, my best friend was ___. Then in eighth grade, my best friend was ___ , and in college, my best friend was ___," and so on. The theme of deep, connecting relationships runs throughout their lives. They use words like *best friend, connection,* and *chemistry* when describing the relationships that energize them the most.

Have you mentioned any names in your life history other than those of your close family members? If you haven't, then you are probably not a *Connecting Core Motivator*.

You might also look at your life and ask yourself whether or not you have the negative or sinful manifestation of *Connecting*. Do you see a theme of *rejecting* in your life? *Connecting Core Motivators* tend to reject people quickly—often in milliseconds. They simply decide a person will not be a connection and they move on. They are done with that person before they ever get to know them.

If you see your life through the lens of people, have had *best friends*, and can easily fall into *rejecting*, then you might be a *Connecting Core Motivator*.

One important note about *Connecting Core Motivators*: *Relational is not Connecting.* We are all relational human beings, but that is not the same as having a specific *Core Motivator* for *Connecting*. Think of it this way, we are all sexual beings, but we are not all sexy. All of us have at some level the desire to engage other people, but a *Connecting Core Motivator* is energized by individual, one-on-one engagements. A *Connecting Core Motivator* sees the whole world through the lens of individual people and is energized by specific one-on-one interactions.

Jack

Jack wants his *Core Motivator* to be *Creating*; in fact, there is some evidence that he is correct. He has built a very successful sales organization and has grown his company from two people to more than fifty in less than five years.

When I looked at Jack's life history, I saw that he began each section with a variation of the following phrase: "When I was in fifth grade my best friend was____." In fact, his whole life was documented in relation to who his best friend was at that time. In what may have been the easiest client session I ever had, I said to him, "Your *Core Motivator* is *Connecting.*" Jack looked at me and said, "It can't be. I'm not good at relationships, and I don't have any." That wasn't true, but his perception of himself was that he didn't have any relationships and that he wasn't good at them. He was in fact so good at them that he took it for granted and did not value his *Core Motivator.*

As we looked at Jack's business, we discovered that he had indeed built his client base one person at a time by connecting with them. They were not just buying his product; they were buying *him.* As we continued to look at his business, we saw that he struggled greatly to dismiss nonperformers because he did not want to endanger his relationship with them. This too is typical of *Connecting Core Motivators* who can be fiercely loyal to their friends because they value those friendships as the highest priority in their life. When Jack embraced his *Core Motivator,* he was able to focus on the key connections that had built his business and dismiss the problem people in his office because he was secure in who he was.

BELONGING

Is your life history filled with the groups you've belonged to? Are the groups or teams you've been a part of the most significant parts of your life? Does your life history read something like this? "When I was in elementary school, I had a great group of friends in the neighborhood. Then in junior high, I was in the Boy Scouts. The best part of high school was being on the football team because of the guys on the team, and the best part of college was my fraternity." If you have the theme of teams and groups, then your *Core Motivator* might be *Belonging.*

Peter

When Peter and I met to discuss his life history, he seemed to always come back to the two football teams he had been on—one in high school, the other in college. As I pursued this subject, we discovered that it wasn't the game of football he liked so much but the camaraderie of being on the team.

As we looked at the rest of his life history, we saw that he viewed all of his life through the lens of the team. His work was about the people on his team, his church was about the small group he was in, and he even viewed his family as his team.

Peter is clearly a *Belonging Core Motivator* and is energized when he is part of or leading a team.

CREATING

If your life history is a recounting of the various projects and tasks you've completed, then your *Core Motivator* might be in one of the five task-oriented *Core Motivator* categories: *Caring, Serving, Giving, Creating,* or *Perfecting.* But before we jump to any conclusions, take a good look at the kinds of tasks you've written about. Are the tasks directed at people?

If there are no names in your life history except perhaps for your wife and children, then you are probably a *Creating Core Motivator.*

If you've written about tasks that don't involve others, then you could be a *Creating Core Motivator*. For example, a *Creating Core Motivator* might write, "The best part of my childhood was that every day in the summer we woke up and built a fort. Then in high school, my favorite thing was the robot I built for the science fair, and in college, it was the computer program I designed." Those tasks do not involve people, and the theme is creating something for the sake of creating it. No other person is necessary to accomplish the task.

Again, it is helpful to look for the negative or sinful themes in your life history. Do you have a history of being judgmental? This is a good indication that your *Core Motivator* might be *Creating*.

It is important to point out that just because a person is creative does not mean they are a *Creating Core Motivator*. Creativity is a gift (refer to the iceberg illustration), but the creative gift is not the same as being a *Creating Core Motivator*. I have met plenty of clients who are *Creating Core Motivators* but are not very creative, and conversely, I have met many creative people who are not *Creating Core Motivators*. For example, you could be a *Connecting Core Motivator* with a gift of creativity.

Note that *Creating Core Motivators* like *Perfecting Core Motivators* tend to be hardest on themselves and those close to them. They tend to apply their judgmental criticism to themselves first and then to those whom they love. They are constantly critical of themselves and their family and trying to recreate them into the people they think they should be. They damage relationships because of their constant criticism, and as a result, they are often left without significant relationships. It is important to recognize this potential problem area and work to live proactively outside of your *Creating* without being judgmental.

Brad

Brad has been a friend for many years. He has been very successful in building key groups of teams in the three different organizations for which he has worked. As we talked about his *Core Motivator*, he was convinced that he was unknowable. He thought that he simply liked his work and had no other *Core Motivator* beyond liking to play with computers. He and his wife had come to visit, and over a period of three days, we talked about what his *Core Motivator* might be.

Finally, as we walked through the mall with our wives on the last night of their visit, Brad and I talked about what was most important in his life. We stopped for dessert, and as the four of us began to talk, he suddenly looked up and said, "Fort! All of life is fort."

He continued, "When I was a kid, we woke up every day in the summer and built a fort. The idea was to build a better fort than the other kids in our neighborhood. That is what my life is about—building better forts." For him, this indeed was what motivated him.

When Brad thinks of his childhood, he doesn't think of the kids in the neighborhood or the sports teams he was on; he thinks of building the fort. Brad moves from one company to another, managing projects. This is what motivates him—what gets him up in the morning. To the extent that Brad can do this, he is happy and motivated. To the extent that he is required to do other things, he is unfulfilled.

Tim is another example of a *Creating Core Motivator*. He is a pastor who was convinced his *Core Motivator* was *Connecting*. I knew he had a *best friend* whom he played golf with and hung out with on a regular basis, so I thought he might be right, but I asked him to write his life history just to be sure.

When I looked at Tim's life history—all twenty pages—there was only one name in the life history: his wife's. He did not mention his friend or even his children by name. When we met, he was adamant that he was a *Connecting Core Motivator*. But after we talked about his life history and the fact that he didn't see his life through the lens of people, he was able to see that he was indeed a *Creating Core Motivator*. He sees the world through the lens of tasks for task's sake.

Tim and Brad both like building things to the extent that when they get to throw themselves into tasks, they are fulfilled. When they are building their forts, they are being the person God made them to be.

If your life history is a collection of tasks, and there are few if any names or people in your life history you might be a *Creating Core Motivator*.

CARING, SERVING, AND GIVING

If your life history is a series of tasks or accomplishments but those tasks are directed at people, then your *Core Motivator* might fall into the middle category (see list in the previous chapter) of *Caring, Serving,* or *Giving*. These *Core Motivators* are tasks directed at people. While a *Creating* or *Perfecting Core Motivator* can accomplish their tasks without people involved, the *Caring, Serving,* and *Giving Core Motivators* need people as the recipients of their tasks, or the task does not make any sense. For example, you can create a desk and you can perfect a desk, but you can't care for a desk, serve a desk, or give to a desk.

The differences between these three *Core Motivators* can be subtle or nuanced, but they are real and important, nonetheless.

CARING

If your life history has a theme of being involved with needy or hurting people, then your *Core Motivator* might be *Caring*. People with this *Core Motivator* often fill their life history with the great things they've done for needy people. They tell about the times they've helped a friend in need or the great needs of the friends they have.

For *Caring Core Motivators*, the negative or sinful manifestation is arrogance. They believe they know what is best for hurting people and that their job is to fix them. This arrogance spills over into every area of their lives. Is there a theme of arrogance in your life history? Did you write sentences like, "I was the best in my school at_____ ," repeatedly in your life history? If so, then you might be a *Caring Core Motivator*.

One interesting thing about this *Core Motivator*—and a warning—is that these people tend to be romantically attracted to needy people because their *Core Motivator* wants to "fix" the other person. They often marry a needy person and then regret that they are "burdened" with that person for the rest of their lives— particularly when they realize they cannot "fix" the person they are married to. If your spouse is needy or you have had a string of relationships with needy people, then your *Core Motivator* might be *Caring*.

Henry

The first thing that jumped off the page as I read Henry's life history was his arrogance. Henry is a great guy with lots of friends; he is beloved by many people. But his close friends will also tell you that he is one of the most arrogant people they know. In his life history, multiple sentences begin with the phrase, "I am the best at _____," or "I was the best in the organization at_____."

Henry is the president of a large organization and has had a successful career, leading several organizations and becoming well-respected in his field. He typically gathers a team of people around him who have a high level of commitment and loyalty. His staff and board of directors love him, but there is always a problem: his teams never seem to produce the kind of results that they should, and he can't seem to keep the best people. While he has done very well, the top job has always eluded him.

As we looked more closely at Henry's life, we saw a pattern in the kinds of teams Henry has built. Throughout his life, Henry has surrounded himself with people who have a common theme of significant personal problems. He is drawn to these types of people. Almost every person on his team has had an issue of hurt and almost debilitating pain. Several are still hurting from the pain of divorce—some have significant physical ailments—others have psychological scars. Henry has taken care of each one and they are fiercely loyal to him.

Henry likes needy people who are hurting, and he gathers them around him to take care of them. They are loyal to him and love him. He thinks his *Core Motivator* is *Creating* because in his life he has built things.

In the course of our meeting together, I asked Henry, "Would you rather be Joe Torre or Don Zimmer?" referring to the famous manager of the New York Yankees and his bench coach. In other words, would you rather be the manager of the team who must walk out to the mound and pull the pitcher or the coach on the bench who consoles the guy after he's been pulled?

Henry's answer was "Zimmer, of course." He doesn't understand why anyone would want to be the guy who must walk out to the mound and pull a pitcher. He sees all of life as finding people whom he can take care of. His *Core Motivator* is *Caring*, and he cares deeply for his staff and board.

Henry faces a double-edged sword of problems. His first problem is that the hurting people are never able to really lead the work he needs to have accomplished because they are significantly restrained by their neediness.

The second—and perhaps more dangerous problem is that Henry doesn't know what to do with healthy people. When people on Henry's team are no longer needy, Henry doesn't know how to lead them, and eventually they leave the team.

The key—and most difficult—thing for *Caring Core Motivators* is to learn the difference between taking care *of* someone and caring *for* someone. Taking care *of* someone assumes that you know what is best for them (arrogance) and that you can be their savior. Caring *for* someone recognizes that only the person can ultimately be responsible for themselves and that you have the privilege of coming alongside them to be part of the healing.

The arrogance assumes that God does not care about the person and is not doing a good job of taking care of them, but you can.

SERVING

People with *Serving* as their *Core Motivator* tend to note in their life history all the ways they've helped other people. The difference between a *Serving Core Motivator* and a *Caring Core Motivator* is that the *Serving Core Motivator* doesn't serve *only* needy people; they will direct their serving tasks to anyone. In this sense, the *task* of serving matters most to those with the *Serving Core Motivator* while the neediness of the *person* matters most to those with the *Caring Core Motivator*.

The *Serving* Core Motivators are the ones you want to help you on a moving day. They love doing that. At their core, they want to serve. It's wonderful, but there is often a downside for them in serving. They can feel taken advantage of and can even begin to feel negative about themselves. They feel weak because they are serving and want to!

One client shared that a friend always calls him for a ride, and he happily accommodates his friend. After a while, he resents being used but at the same time is deeply gratified and energized by being used. He sometimes hates his friend for using him and hates himself for liking being used. This is difficult for *Serving Core Motivators* to navigate, and they must learn to strike a balance between healthy serving and not being taken advantage of.

Serving Core Motivators also tend to have three qualities that identify them. First, they tend to place discipline as the highest value in their lives. They care more about their personal discipline than anything else. Second, they have rarely cried in their life. Part of their discipline is to not show emotion. I have a friend who is a *Serving Core Motivator* who never cries. He didn't even cry at his wife's funeral! Third they tend to be exercise fanatics. Another part of their discipline is they exercise obsessively to have control over their bodies.

The negative or sinful manifestation of the *Serving Core Motivator* is pride. The *Serving Core Motivator* looks at what he or she does for others and thinks, "I am pretty special. Look at all the good things I've done for people." They are also proud of themselves for their discipline.

Tim

Tim's life history was an accounting of the great things he had done to help other people. He had been part of a project to help underprivileged kids when he was in grade school and then a mission trip in high school. The list went on and on.

The thing that really stood out for me when I read Tim's story was the amazing amount of pride he took in each task. When I asked him about the various projects he had been involved in, his face lit up when he mentioned things he had built for people or the times when he had gone out of his way to do something for someone. He was hard-pressed to remember the people specifically, but he remembered with great detail the tasks he had done to help them.

If your life history has a theme of "look at how great I am" and if discipline is your highest value and you've never cried and you are obsessed with exercise, then you might have the *Core Motivator* of *Serving*.

GIVING

People who have the *Core Motivator* of *Giving* will write their life histories with the theme of the times they have given to others or to organizations in various ways. They are benefactors. *Giving* tends to fall into two categories: material things (money, objects and more) and advice.

The negative or sinful manifestation of *Giving* is a kind of paternalistic haughtiness. The definition of haughty is a combination of pride and arrogance. If you are energized by the activity of giving—whether it is financially or otherwise and you tend to look down on other people, then your *Core Motivator* might be *Giving*.

Alice

When Alice and I met, she had just been downsized from an investment firm. She had both an MBA and a law degree and was highly qualified for the job, but her boss never liked her. When the cash flow got tight, she was let go.

Alice is a nice person and a strong person. She wants to tell you everything she knows, but not in an arrogant way. She is more like an excited puppy that wants to lick your face whether you want it to or not. She is effusive.

Her life history is filled with damaged relationships and job losses. She is quite a wonderful person, but there is something unsettling about being around her. As we looked at her life history, we saw that she was always the advice giver—the person everyone came to for advice in junior high and the sorority sister who was the confidant of the sisterhood. She gives advice to her parents, siblings, and anyone else who will listen to her—which is a dwindling crowd.

As we dug more deeply into her compulsion to give advice, we saw that she was not as interested in the actual advice itself as she was in the thrill of giving it to another person. It was the giving that energized her. But her boss didn't want advice from her. He was confident in his own wisdom and wanted her to do her job, not tell him how to do his. The combination of her aggressive, quick-to-advise nature and the haughty attitude that came with it made her an easy target to dislike.

The key for Alice was to learn when advice was wanted and when it was not. She had to learn when to give and when not to give. Her next job—where she was very successful and appreciated—was one in which her boss valued her advice, asked for her advice, and needed her advice.

Exercise Number 4: Talk to Your Spouse and Friends

After you have analyzed your life history and thought about what your *Core Motivator* might be, it's time to test your thesis. Sit down with a couple of people who know you well and ask them what they think. You may be surprised how much insight other people can provide for you.

When I first started working with clients, I had a picture of a secluded retreat center where people would process their life history, take long walks in the woods, and ponder the deep things of their lives. What I found was that people were busy and didn't want to travel to Canada to work on themselves, so I went to them. What I discovered was that as people completed the first day of the process—discovering their *Core Motivators*—they would go home and discuss it with their spouse, who inevitably confirmed for them what we had discovered.

Pam

Pam called me because she was going to retire early and didn't know what she would do with the rest of her life. She'd had a tremendous career with a major Fortune 500 company, rising through the ranks to assume great responsibility and reporting directly to the chairman. When the chairman—Pam's mentor and advocate—decided to retire in a year, Pam wanted to leave also.

As we began our session, I asked her (as I do all clients) what she thought her *Core Motivator* was. She told me she was sure it was *Caring*, but she was still interested in the discovery process.

As we began to work through her life history, we found little evidence of the theme of *Caring*. We saw that Pam was a task-oriented person who owed much of her corporate success to her ability to take on new projects and create successful ventures for the company. No one could clean up a mess and start something new better than Pam.

When I suggested to her that the theme of her life—and her *Core Motivator*—was *Creating*, she was less than thrilled. After we had debated the issue for a couple of hours, she agreed to think about it more and talk to some of her closest friends, and we ended the session.

When we met the next morning, Pam told me that she had spent the evening calling her closest friends and sister to explain the process and my conclusions. Each person agreed with me and told her that there was no way her *Core Motivator* was *Caring*. She was devastated—and free. On one hand, she was not happy that she was not as caring a person as she had thought. She had been told all of her life that to be a good mother and wife she had to be a caring person, and she was trying very hard to be that nurturing, caring woman. The problem was it just wasn't who she was. On the other hand, she was thrilled to finally have permission to be who she really is.

Your friends may know you better than you know yourself.

As you process your life history, there is great value in having your friends help you see what you may not otherwise be able to recognize.

Here is a chart with each of the Core Motivators, their primary characteristic, and their negative (sinful) manifestation. As you look at the chart it is sometimes helpful to ask the following questions:

1. *Which Core Motivator do I think I am? (You can probably cross this one off the list; it's probably not your Core Motivator.)*
2. *Which Core Motivator do I like the least? (Take this one seriously. There is a strong chance this is your Core Motivator.)*
3. *Which negative or sinful manifestation most resonates with me? This is another good clue as to your Core Motivator.*

Core Motivator Chart

Core Motivator	Characteristic	Negative Manifestation
Connecting	One-on-one connections	Rejecting
Belonging	Groups/teams	People pleasing
Caring	Attracted to needy people	Arrogance
Serving	Energized by people's needs	Pride
Giving	What can I give you?	Haughty
Creating	What can I create?	Judgmental
Perfecting	How can I make it perfect?	Perfectionism

EXERCISE NUMBER 5: ORDERING THE CORE MOTIVATOR

Once you have discovered what your *Core Motivator* is, you can also take some time to put the list of *Core Motivators* in an order that reflects their magnitude in your life. When I do this, I make a list of ten, leaving numbers 2, 3, and 4 blank to show the great gulf between your first and true —*Core Motivator* and your second. It is helpful to know your first, second (fifth on the list), and tenth (last on the list) *Core Motivators.*

Your first *Core Motivator* is the one that matters most and is the one that you will base on when you build your vision. It is helpful to know your second because most of us are tempted to live out of our second instead of our first. We see our first as weak and default to our second, so it's helpful to know our second *Core Motivator* and be aware of that temptation.

It is also helpful to see what is last on our list. Your *Core Motivator* is the lens through which you see all of life and you do not see life at all through the lens that is the last *Core Motivator.* I am reminded of the comment from an eye surgeon who said, "Most people think blind people see black, but actually they don't *see* at all." With our last *Core Motivator*, we don't see at all.

My last *Core Motivator* is *Serving*, and when my son offered the carpet guy a glass of water (page 50), I hadn't seen it at all. I was blind to it. Knowing our last *Core Motivator* helps us understand what we are blind to and that we need other people in our lives who can take us by the hand and lead us to those places we can't see. In other words, I need my son to tell me, "Dad, this guy needs a glass of water."

This is part of why we need to understand our *Core Motivator* and that of the people we work with. The best teams know the part each *Core Motivator* plays in making the team successful. They know who sees what through their lens and who is blind. This is key information for effective teams and can be the difference between success and failure for a team.

CORE MOTIVATOR LIST

1. *Your Core Motivator—who you truly are at your core.*
2. _ _ _ _ _ _ _ _ _ _
3. _ _ _ _ _ _ _ _ _ _
4. _ _ _ _ _ _ _ _ _ _
5. *Your second—you are tempted to live here.*
6. *Your third*
7. *Your fourth*
8. *Your fifth*
9. *Your sixth*
10. *Your last—you are blind to this. You don't see this at all.*

Chapter 11

CHANGING THE PARADIGM OF SELF

And when I am weak, then I am strong.
—2 Corinthians 12:10

"There are too many posers around," the skateboarder said to me.

"What?" I replied, confused by his comment.

The young man who had made that statement was an excellent skateboarder at a time when skateboarding was at the height of its popularity. He was looking around at a bunch of kids who were dressing like skateboarders and wearing their hair like them. He called them posers because they were pretending to be something they weren't. They were posing as skateboarders, but they didn't know how to skate at all.

In my work, I've met a lot of posers—people who are trying to be someone they're not. I've met a lot of men who have spent most of their lives trying to be tougher than they are and a lot of women who aren't sure if they should be tougher or weaker. When we aren't comfortable with who we are at our core, we develop a false self that is a poor representation of who we wish we were rather than who we actually are. We work hard at developing that false self, and we have a lot of people convinced that we are someone we're not. Typically, the false self is built on the "second" *Core Motivator* because we are deceived into thinking it is better/stronger than our true *Core Motivator*.

Often, we become so comfortable with the facade we've created—living out of the second—that we're frightened by the thought of abandoning that false self and living out of who we really are. Our false self creates our comfort zone for living—a place where we don't feel exposed—and none of us wants the risk of exposing the real person at our core since we ourselves are afraid to face that person. But that place is not really good for us because it is a false sense of comfort, and it prevents us from being all of who we really are.

When we create an alternate persona, we do so for a reason. We are afraid the real person—the one hiding beneath the false self—will be rejected or fail if exposed. Therefore, we are unwilling to dispose of the characters we have created and allow our true selves—the persons that God created—to come forth. We are like a trapeze artist, afraid to let go of the first swing for fear that the next might be unattainable, afraid we will fall.

When my son was young, we decided to have his birthday party at a local pizza place. It was a mom-and-pop version of Chucky Cheese, and its mascot was a dinosaur. We gathered the hyperenergetic boys at the restaurant to play games, run around, eat pizza, and have a great time.

Our waitress was a young woman in her early twenties who had a bad attitude. She wasn't nasty; she just wasn't excited about serving us. She shuffled over to our table with her shoulders slumped, didn't make eye contact, and dropped our menus on the table before shuffling away.

About thirty minutes later, it was time for the dinosaur to appear and bring the birthday boy his cake. We immediately recognized the person inside the dino outfit as our waitress. The slumped shoulders, the shuffling gait, and the I-wish-I-was-anywhere-but-here attitude gave her away. She could put on a dinosaur costume, but she was still the same disgruntled employee.

Many of us live the same way. We may have put on a different costume—the costume of our second *Core Motivator*—but others can still see the person inside the costume for who we are. The only person we're fooling is our self.

Ned

I mentioned Ned in chapter 7. You may recall that when I met with him, I asked him to describe his childhood. He explained that he'd had an allergy that caused him to have a physical impediment, which caused his classmates to view him as a nerd. To compensate for this rejection by his peers, he developed an alternate persona: the class clown.

As the court jester of his class, Ned was willing to make a fool of himself to get laughs. Like any school kid, he wanted to belong, and he contorted himself to do whatever it took to belong. Because of his silliness, he achieved a certain degree of acceptance among his peers, and he was welcomed into a group of friends. When he eventually became one of the popular kids, he found himself mocking other kids instead of being mocked. Success? Not really. Ned was now living out of his second *Core Motivator* of *Belonging*, but he was not being the true person God had created him to be.

When I worked with Ned in his late twenties, he had just been fired by the owner of a small restaurant. The owner of the restaurant told him, "You are wasting your life here, and I won't be part of it." That was a great owner!

Ned didn't know who he was. He was trying to be a *Belonging Core Motivator*, still in his late twenties, and he was paralyzed. Ned's true *Core Motivator* is *Creating*, and today he is an artistic director at a large public relations firm. Now he wakes up every day energized by living out of his *Core Motivator*.

The persona he developed had served him well—or so he thought. The only problem was that the person his friends had accepted—and the person Ned had made himself into—wasn't the real Ned. The class clown persona was simply the character Ned had created and was living through. In order for Ned to live out of who God created him to be, he first had to rediscover the little boy he had been in fourth grade and accept that kid. He had to realize that God created that little boy and loved him. Ned had to learn to love that little boy too.

But we can see in Ned that his true *Core Motivator* was at work. He created the new Ned. Even though he thought he was living out of a *Belonging Core Motivator*, the reality was in clear sight if anyone was looking for it. Ned sees life through the lens of what he can create, and he has created a new Ned.

Ned's root problem was that he—like all of us—wanted to play the role of God. Ned wanted to remake himself. He looked at God's creation (himself) and made a judgment on that creation, deciding that God hadn't done a very good job of creating Ned and that he (Ned) could do a better job. Ned looked in the mirror at the raw material he'd been handed and decided to recreate himself to be more acceptable to his peers.

The recreated Ned was something like New Coke, in that it sounded like a good idea and was remade to compete with the previous version of itself. Like New Coke, new Ned was a failure. He wasn't initially a failure; the problem came as he matured because he didn't know the joy of being the true person God created. As the years caught up with him, Ned spent his life in frustration, always trying to attain satisfaction but never succeeding.

You see, Ned's second *Core Motivator* could never be all that God intended him to be. It could be only a weak imitation of the person God created. Ned found himself paralyzed—unable to be himself—because he didn't know who he was.

We Want to Be like God

The root sin of Adam and Eve was that they wanted to be like God. They couldn't accept who they were. They wanted to be like someone else. They wanted to be like God. When Adam and Eve were tempted in the garden, the serpent said, "You will not surely die. For God knows that in the day you eat of it (the fruit of the tree) your eyes will be opened, and *you will be like God* [italics mine], knowing good and evil."

The sin that infected Adam and Eve—one that has been passed on to all of us—is that we want to be like God.

When we put on a false persona (the one we think will work for us), we are usurping God's creative work in us. While it is true that, as image bearers of God, we have the ability to create, the ultimate author of creation is God. When we usurp God's creative supremacy, we fall into the same sinful behavior that cursed Adam and Eve. Most of us fall into this trap. We don't like what God has created in us, so we attempt to recreate ourselves in the image we perceive will fit best into the world around us. This recreation becomes the demise of our true selves.

Ron

Ron came to me faced with a big decision. He was an attorney in the armed services who hated everything about his career. He was in a secure position and was being promoted to greater and greater responsibility, yet he wanted to give it all up to stock shelves at the local grocery store.

Ever since Ron was very young, he had been working to prove he was tough. He had been a leader among his peers and had become an Eagle Scout. After graduating from college, he didn't know what to do, so he applied to law school. After three days of law school, he knew he hated it, but he wasn't going to be a quitter. He stuck it out.

He decided to prove he was strong and tough, so he stayed in law school and finished. He never had any passion for law or justice or even winning; he stayed simply because he could not bring himself to quit.

When Ron finished law school, the military was recruiting on campus, so he signed up. Again, this decision was made not because of any passion for the military but because he didn't have a passion for anything else. The military would give him another venue in which to prove his toughness.

As we discussed Ron's life, we discovered that his *Core Motivator* is *Serving*. What Ron loves to do most is give food to the poor and work with street people. This energizes him. It brings out the real Ron.

Ron had spent most of his life creating his tough guy persona and living out of his second *Core Motivator—Creating—*because he hated the feeling of perceived weakness that he saw in *Serving*. At thirty-seven years of age, the lie had caught up with him. He wanted to leave his job as a military lawyer and stock shelves at the grocery store. He was ready to give up on life.

As he began to understand who he was—both his true self and the alternate persona he created based on his second *Core Motivator*—he was ready to face the real Ron and begin to be himself.

Ron and Ned made a classic mistake that many of us make. They thought that by hiding their weaknesses, they could be strong. But the apostle Paul said, "When I am weak then I am strong." When Paul faced his weakness, then and only then could he be strong. In fact, when we are trying to be strong, we are actually at our weakest point.

Ron is weakest when he is trying to be the tough military attorney because it's not really him. Ned is weakest when he is trying to be the *belonger* because that is not really who he is. Ron is strongest when he is serving people. When he serves his clients, he is at his best. Ned is strongest when he is using his *Creating Core*

Motivator to design marketing campaigns. The paradox of our lives is that when we are weak, then we are strong.

Bob

When I was about a year into my first staff assignment, my predecessor came to me one day and said, "Bob, the Bible says to speak the truth in love. You have a lot of truth but not much love." I was taken aback by his comment and appreciated him saying it to me. But he was wrong on both accounts. I didn't have that much truth, but I did have a lot more love than I was willing to show.

When I had the idea of a *Core Motivator* the first thing I did was share the idea with my best friend. We met for a weekend to discuss the idea and see if it had any substance to it. As we talked, he told me that my *Core Motivator* was relationships. (This was before we had begun the process, and today, we call that *Connecting*.) I was sure my *Core Motivator* was something like evangelism or strategy (this was before I realized those weren't *Core Motivators*, and today I would have said *Creating)*, and I was offended that he would accuse me of being so weak. When I heard the word relationships, I heard weakness.

He said, "You do ministry out of relationships." I felt exposed and I became defensive. I didn't want anyone to see that part of me, and I had been trying (unsuccessfully) to hide that for years. I was angry and upset. We argued for the better part of a day, and by dinner, we weren't even speaking. How could he tell me who I was?

We went to a movie, and when I came out of the theatre, I stopped in the street and said to my friend, "I think you're right. I think my *Core Motivator* is relationships. How do I not know who I am?"

For *years* I had been living out of a false self—my second *Core Motivator* of *Creating*—and I didn't even know it. I had been trying to be a lot tougher than I was, and like the girl in the dinosaur costume, my friend was able to see the real me under the cover of my posing as a tough guy.

I am learning every day what it means to embrace what I used to perceive as my weakness, learning to be *proactively weak* because I know that I am most fulfilled in life when I am being the person God made me to be. I know now the truth of the apostle's statement, "When I am weak then I am strong."

Side note: Most men think their *Core Motivator* is weak, and when presented with the list of seven *Core Motivators*, they choose *Creating* because it seems to be the most masculine one on the list. Conversely most women want their *Core Motivator* to be *Caring* because it seems to be the most maternal on the list.

There is good news for all of us. God didn't err when He made us. We were created in His image, and He wants us to live as the person He intended us to be, not as a poser. It may seem counterintuitive, but as we embrace what we perceive to be our weakness—the *Core Motivator* we think is the weakest—then we will find our strength. It is in being fully the person God created us to be that we'll become strong.

THE VALUE OF THE PERSON

Part of the reason we try to recreate who we are is that we don't understand where our value as a person comes from. In the last fifty years, there has been a massive effort in our culture to enhance the self-image of individuals in our society. Many of our society's ills have been blamed on a poor self-image among our citizens. We have attempted to correct this problem by trying to convince people that they are good. We hope that if they feel better about themselves, they will become better citizens.

Jeffrey Dahmer was a sick individual. He kidnapped little children, sexually abused them, killed them, and even practiced cannibalism. After he was convicted and sent to prison, he had a pen pal. In an article in *Time* magazine, his pen pal said that Jeffrey was basically a good person. My question is, based on what criteria? Why does our culture demand that in spite of clear evidence to the contrary, we have to tell ourselves that there is something good about Jeffrey Dahmer?

Our culture also associates our values with what we do or what we produce. We have come to believe that people are valuable based on how well they perform in a certain arena. This method of assessment has devastating results when we value our children based on their grades or athletic performance. It has even more tragic results when we value ourselves based on what we accomplish. If we wake up one day and realize we haven't accomplished very much, we may then feel worthless. We have made the mistake of basing our value on our achievements.

We live in a toxic cocktail—a mix of being told that we are all good people blended with the idea that our goodness comes from what we achieve. The reasoning goes even further to conclude that if we embrace our goodness, we'll be able to accomplish more, and as we accomplish more, then we will be more highly valued. However, the social fabricators have realized that not everyone achieves at the same level, so they have decided that the enemy is competition. In many areas of life (especially those concerning children), there are no winners or losers anymore; everyone wins. Today in some Little League baseball games, after the game, all the participants get medals because we wouldn't want anyone to feel badly about themselves. This is a failed philosophy that doesn't work as we see self-esteem issues become even greater in our culture. Even a six-year-old boy knows that just because everyone gets a medal, that doesn't mean everyone is a winner.

Sometimes we even think about God in this way. Does God like us only when we are good or because of our list of great accomplishments and good deeds? The Bible tells us He does not base His love for us on our achievements.

Basing our worth on our accomplishments and good deeds is

an anti-biblical model. To begin with, Jesus said that no one is good except God (Mark 10:18). Second the Bible teaches that God doesn't approve of us because of our accomplishments or works. In fact, the biblical perspective is that the only work acceptable to God is the work of Christ on the cross—not our work but His.

Where then does our worth come from? If we aren't valuable because of our works or any goodness inherent in us, then why does God value us?

Michelangelo gives us a great example of the answer to this question. His statue of David stands in a specially designed domed room in the National Museum of Bargello in Florence, Italy. When you enter this museum, you walk down a short hall and make a right turn into another hall. Several uncompleted statues line this second hall, which is the entryway to the masterpiece. These partially carved pieces of marble are statues that Michelangelo began to sculpt but for one reason or another, stopped working on. They are not great works of art, yet they are priceless. Their value comes from the one who put his chisel to them—the great artist Michelangelo. They are not good, but they are of immeasurable value.

You and I are like those imperfect hunks of marble. We aren't valuable because we are good or because of our good works. We are priceless because the God of the universe put His hand on us when He created us and breathed His life into us. We are His creation, and as such, we are more valuable than anything we could make ourselves.

We must learn to find our true value in the fact that we have been created by God, that He has made us in His image, and that He loves us. We are not like Michelangelo's *David*—a perfect specimen. We are much more like the unfinished statues in the hall. We are imperfect, broken, and unfinished people, waiting for the day when we will be made perfect. But for now, in this life and in this time, we must embrace our weakness—our imperfection—and rejoice in the knowledge that we are created in the image of God who loves us. This is where we will find our value and the security of a healthy self-image—not in our flaws but in our creator.

Chapter 12

THE STAR: CHANGING THE PARADIGM OF PURPOSE

And the star which they had seen in the
east, went on before them.
—Matthew 2:9

I n this chapter, we are going to discuss the concept of a navigation point—what I refer to as a Star—and how we can define a Star for our lives. I often tell clients that discovering your *Core Motivator* can be painful and setting your Star can be difficult, but if you get those two things right, then setting the Mountains is easy.

WHAT IS A STAR?

FOR THE PURPOSE OF BUILDING A VISION FOR YOUR LIFE, A STAR IS A NAVIGATION POINT. IT IS A POINT IN THE DISTANCE THAT YOU WILL NEVER REACH, BUT IT GIVES YOU SOMETHING TO AIM FOR.

DRIVING TO COLORADO

Many years ago, my wife and I drove from our home in St. Louis to visit my sister in Colorado. We drove through the flat terrain of Kansas and Eastern Colorado until finally in the distance we could see the peaks of the Rocky Mountains. As we drew closer, there spread before us as far as we could see to our left and to our right were the extended arms of the Rocky Mountains.

Imagine stopping at that point and getting out of your car to take in the grandeur of this majestic sight. Also imagine that you wanted to do some mountain climbing and that you were trying to decide which particular mountain in that vast range to climb. It would be helpful if you had a navigational point that you could follow—a point that would show you the way.

For centuries, navigators used stars to guide them on their journeys. Early sailors used the North Star (some 680 light-years away) as a reference point for guidance when navigating the high seas. The wise men also used a star to guide them to the baby Jesus. In both cases, the star the travelers followed wasn't their goal; it simply pointed them in the right direction.

The same is true for us. We will set a Star that gives us direction and points us down the right path.

A star is a point of light in space. Actually, science tells us that a star is a celestial body that is so far away that it appears to be a small point of light. Yet this small point of light can give us direction, and it is this directional use of a star that is illustrative for us now.

When we talk of a Star in the process of *building a Vision for Your Life,* we are referring to a statement that will serve as a navigational point in setting our vision. We are talking about a point that is so far away from us that we will never reach it, yet it guides us and gives us direction. The purpose of this Star is to serve as a guiding point rather than an end point. It is not our intention to reach the Star; rather we are going to set a Star so that we have two points: our *Core*

Motivator and our Star. Between these two points, we will be able to draw a straight line, which we will call our life path.

The Coca-Cola Company once stated in an annual report that it wanted to be the provider of every ounce of liquid consumed in the world. That is a great Star. This statement gives the company an unattainable point at which to aim. It helps define the mission and the business. I don't think Coca-Cola imagines that it could actually *be* the sole provider of every ounce of liquid consumed, including every drop of water and every cup of tea. That is one of the reasons this is such a great Star because Coca-Cola is in the thirst-quenching business, not just the soda pop business. By defining its Star this way, Coke has set a point that is unattainable yet keeps the focus on its core business.

There are four guidelines for setting the right Star for your life. They are

1. *the Star must be so large it is unattainable,*
2. *the Star must flow from the Core Motivator,*
3. *the Star must focus the Core Motivator on a particular passion, and*
4. *the Star must have an ultimate purpose.*

STEP 1: THE SIZE OF THE STAR

The size of the Star is a key principle in setting a Star for your life. For a Star to be a Star, remember that it is a point that may look small from where you stand, but in reality, it is very large. Scientists tell us that our sun is a small star, so imagine what the size of the other stars must be!

The first step in defining a Star is, to begin with the premise that your Star must be a huge point in the distance. The idea of a small Star is an oxymoron. In writing your Star Statement, I suggest you include words that will force you to think in ways far beyond what you could ever accomplish. For example, when the Star involves the whole world or even the whole universe, then its scope has been defined as widely as possible. I suggest you include the phrase "the whole world" in your Star because this will force you to think outside your comfort zone and beyond what you could easily accomplish right now.

STEP 2: INCORPORATE YOUR CORE MOTIVATOR

The second step in defining a Star for your life is to extrapolate from your *Core Motivator* what kind of Star you are to plot. For example, if your *Core Motivator* is *Serving*, then your Star must involve serving in a large, far-reaching way. You might begin with a phrase something like "Serving the whole world." Or if your *Core Motivator* is *Caring*, you might include the phrase, "Caring for every person in the world." Another example would be for a *Core Motivator* of *Creating*, the Star could include "Creating works that will impact the whole world." In this way, you have connected your *Core Motivator* to the furthest possibilities of what might be accomplished.

STEP 3: IDENTIFY YOUR PASSION

The third step in creating your Star is defining your passion. This is the step most of us struggle with since we are at a loss to define our passion.

Passion, like great art, begins in our minds. What we think about is what we become, and what we are passionate about is what we will do. As I mentioned earlier, Michelangelo lived a passionate kind of life. His work was congruent with who he was, and he lived his life out of his passion for creating great art. He didn't define his job and build his life into his work; rather his life was defined by his passion, and then his various jobs were built into his life.

One evening when I was having dinner with a friend, we began to talk about the *Vision for Your Life* process. I asked him a question I've asked many people during this process. The question was "What would you do every day if money were no object?" My friend thought for a few moments and finally said, "I have no idea what I'd do every day if money were no object."

We continued to eat our dinner and talk about other things. About an hour later, he said to me, "It's pretty scary that I don't know what I'd do. It means I don't know myself very well. I don't even know what I like to do."

I agree. That is scary, but my friend is not alone. This lack of self-knowledge is the reality for most of us. We don't know ourselves well enough to know what we'd do with our lives if we didn't have to focus on earning money.

I once asked a group of twenty-five men to fill out the day schedule sheet if money was no object. Only one of them had any idea what he would do (and he was in a position where money was indeed no object for him). Sure, we all dream of winning the lottery, traveling around the world, buying the car of our dreams, and picking out vacation property—but then what? Why do so few of us know what we would do with our lives if we had all the money we needed? Is it because money is the primary motivator for our lives? Is it because we've never asked the question?

Or might it be that the answer to the question seems too scary for us to think about? Perhaps we don't think about what we'd do with our lives if money were no object because we're afraid. We fear that if we didn't have any financial needs, we wouldn't have any goals at all.

EXERCISE NUMBER 6: WHAT WOULD YOUR DAY LOOK LIKE?

At this point in our process, I want you to take a few minutes and respond to the same question I posed to my friend at dinner. Below you will find an empty day schedule. Fill it out as if money were no object. In other words, what would you do with every day if money wasn't a factor in deciding how you would spend your time? You should be as specific as possible. Assume you will begin your day by getting out of bed, taking a shower, eating breakfast, reading the paper, and then what? What will you do next?

In asking this question, I am not talking about what episodic experiences you would undertake—the world travel, the shopping sprees, and the days spent playing golf. These are only temporary events. I am asking what your life would look like every day if money wasn't a constraining issue in your life.

Take a few minutes now and jot down your answer to this question. Try to be as specific as possible, painting in the details of your picture as best you can. Once you have written your initial response, take some time to reflect on this picture and ask yourself, "Is this what I would really do with my life if money were not a concern?" Let this question and its response roll over in your mind for a day or two until you come to peace with the picture you have created. Then come back to this section.

If money were no object, here is how I would spend my day:

6:00 a.m._____

7:00 a.m._____

8:00 a.m._____

9:00 a.m._____

10:00 a.m._____

11:00 a.m._____

12:00 p.m._____

1:00 p.m._____

2:00 p.m._____

3:00 p.m._____

4:00 p.m._____

5:00 p.m._____

6:00 p.m._____

7:00 p.m._____

8:00 p.m._____

9:00 p.m._____

*10:00 p.m.*_____

_____

*11:00 p.m.*_____

_____

*12:00 a.m.*_____

_____

Exercise Number 7: What Would Your Ideal Year Look Like?

Here is a similar exercise. Think about your life as a series of one-year events. Now envision those one-year events as a clock with each hour representing a month. You can go either clockwise or counterclockwise but try to fill in the clock as if money were no object. Where would holidays fit on your clock? Where would time for travel, study, and work each fit on your clock? What would your ideal year look like?

*1. January*_____

_____

*2. February*_____

_____

*3. March*_____

_____

4. *April*_____

_____

5. *May*_____

_____

6. *June*_____

_____

7. *July*_____

_____

8. *August*_____

_____

9. *September*_____

_____

10. *October*_____

_____

11. *November*_____

_____

12. *December*_____

_____

WHAT IS YOUR PASSION?

The purpose of these two exercises is to begin to get a picture of what your passions are. You can look at your day and see what you are passionate about. Is your day filled with physical activity? Your passion might be exactly that. Is your day filled with creating works of art? Your passion might be art. Is your day filled with study? Your passion might be learning, knowledge, or truth. When you look at your day what is the passion you see?

Look at your year and see what themes are there. Is there a theme of travel or adventure? Then to what end do you travel or seek adventure? Is there a theme of work? What kind of work? To what end?

These exercises give you a clue to what you are passionate about, and you need to peel away the surface (I like to travel) and ask what is the depth of that (I travel to experience other cultures).

You should also see your *Core Motivator* in your day and month exercises. If you don't see that, then you might want to return to the exercise and be more proactive about plotting your day and year with your *Core Motivator*.

By the same token if all you see in your day and month is your *Core Motivator* then you should dig deeper to ask, "To what end am I doing my *Core Motivator*?" For example, if your day is filled with one-on-one meetings, and you are a *Connecting Core Motivator*, that is good. But you need to ask the deeper question, "What are those connections about? What is happening in those meetings?"

Or, if your *Core Motivator* is *Creating* and your year is filled with various projects, that is great. But you need to ask deeper questions like, "What kind of projects—to what end?"

Again, as in looking for your *Core Motivator*, you are looking for themes. For example, if there is a theme of reading and study, then perhaps your passion lies somewhere in the area of academia. Perhaps the theme of your day and year is involvement with people; your passion might be engaging people in one form or another. Another possibility might be that your day and year are filled with physical activities—hiking, skiing, camping, and so on, and your passion is for the outdoors or physical exercise.

When you look at your day and year pages, what themes do you see, and what is really behind those themes? For example, if you have a passion for the outdoors, then to what purpose is that passion directed? Is it for other people to experience nature, or is it for you to experience it alone?

If you can identify your passion as involving other people, then you need to ask, "To what end am I meeting with people?" Is your desire to meet with people to lead them in a certain direction? If so, then your Star statement might include that direction.

If you can identify your passion as an academic exercise, then you need to ask, "To what end am I pursuing academics? What is the end goal of my studying?" The answer to that question will be the passion part of your star.

STEP 4: ULTIMATE PURPOSE

The fourth step in setting a Star involves centering your life on something greater than yourself. For some of us, the grand purpose of our lives is to glorify God. For others, our grand purpose is to live our lives to the fullest. In either case, these are good phrases to add to complete your Star statement.

EXERCISE NUMBER 8: CONSTRUCTING THE STAR STATEMENT

Once you have chosen a statement that is unattainable (the whole world), have identified your *Core Motivator* and passion, and can state your ultimate purpose, you are ready to construct your Star statement.

You should begin constructing your Star statement with either the phrase, "I will glorify God by ..." or "I will live my life to the fullest by ..." then add in your *Core Motivator*, followed by your passion, and finally ending with your unattainable phrase.

For example, you can say, "I will glorify God by serving the poor and eliminating hunger in the world," or "I will live my life to the fullest by serving the poor and eliminating hunger in the world."

Let's say your passion is music, and your *Core Motivator* is *Creating.* Your Star statement might be "I will glorify God by creating music for the whole world to enjoy." The elements of glorifying God, your *Core Motivator*, and your specific interest are coming together to form a unique Star that will give you a good guiding point.

Examples of Star Statements from clients:

I will glorify God by connecting with every person in the whole world bringing them the truth.

I will live my life to the fullest by caring for the entire world and coaching them one person at a time.

I will glorify God by belonging to teams that extend God's grace to the whole world.

I will glorify God by serving every person in the whole world, meeting them where they are, in order for them to grow spiritually.

I will glorify God by giving prophetic guidance to the world so that all may experience the wonder, joy, and fullness of life.

I will live my life to the fullest by creating fun experiences that cause the whole world to lighten up.

I will glorify God by perfecting the details that make the whole world work better.

Throughout your life, your Star should not change, but you might begin to describe it with more clarity and specificity. As you become more in touch with your *Core Motivator* and the truth of who God has created you to be, you will become better at describing the details of your Star.

Chapter 13

MOUNTAINS: CHANGING THE PARADIGM OF GOALS

Begin with the end in mind.
—Stephen Covey

A t this point in our process we must ask the question, "How will building a vision affect my daily life?" If what you are doing in this process of building a vision for your life doesn't have an effect on how you live, then it isn't particularly valuable.

In this chapter, we're going to look at your *life path*—the line between your *Core Motivator* and your star—and begin to define specific points along that path. Once we have defined this life path, then we'll look at the specific tasks to be accomplished.

.   Our goal now is to establish specific and accomplishable goals. I call these goals mountains. Mountains are the specific goals or benchmarks you want to accomplish in your life. The most important thing to remember when setting benchmarks is that they must be consistent with your *Core Motivator* and your Star Statement.

If we return to our Eastern Colorado illustration, you now know point A—your *Core Motivator*, and point B—your Star. These two points give you a straight line that shows you which Mountains to climb.

With that picture in mind, we are going to begin with the biggest, most distant goal we can imagine. We are going to pick the farthest mountaintop we can see and set our sights on climbing that Mountain. The key to this exercise is to pick the right mountain range based on your personal Star because you will be striving for this Mountain range your whole life. The road up that mountain range is called your *life path*.

Back to Eastern Colorado, looking at the Rocky Mountains, you can see only the very top of the most distant mountain. You know it is there, and you know it is gray, but you don't know much else about it. The same is true for your furthest *life Mountain*. You know it is there, and you know you will be older when you reach it, but you may not know much else about it. That's OK. The point is that you are beginning even now to consider how to climb that Mountain.

EXERCISE NUMBER 9: SETTING MOUNTAINS

Stephen Covey has famously said that we need to "begin with the end in mind." If you begin with the end in mind, then you have a better chance of drawing the right strategy for accomplishing your goals. It is helpful at this point in the process of goal setting, then for us to begin with the most distant Mountain we can see.

Once again, we will turn to Michelangelo. He finished his final statue eight days before his death at eighty-nine years of age. What would your Mountain look like at eighty-nine years old, keeping in mind that you want it to be on the path to your Star?

I want you to paint a mental picture of what you would like to be doing when you are eighty-nine years old. In other words, what would you want your life to look like when you're eighty-nine? What would your life look like on a daily basis, knowing the importance of being involved in significant work? What do you want to be doing? Envision yourself at eighty-nine—fully engaged in your life's work—and describe that picture as clearly as you can.

This is the first Mountain we should look at—the one furthest away. For the sake of this exercise, we'll call it your "eighty-nine-year Mountain." As you think about this Mountain and begin to describe it, make sure this Mountain is aligned with your Star. In other words, make sure it is part of what you already know you want your whole life to be about.

Because your eighty-nine-year Mountain is far away and you won't be able to make out the details of the terrain, we are only asking a general question here. We are only trying to describe what you can see from where you are now. But at least you are looking at the Mountain. There may not be much to see from here, but you are describing what you do see. That is a giant step in the right direction.

It may be helpful to think about your last days at eighty-nine years old and ask, "What would I have wanted my life to look like?" One easy starting place is to rephrase your Star statement as your eighty-nine-year Mountain. For example, if your Star statement is *I will glorify God by connecting with every person in the whole world bringing them the truth,* then your eighty-nine-year Mountain might be something like "At eighty-nine, I will have connected with and engaged the world with truth."

Another good element of the eighty-nine Mountain is to think about the commitments you've made to your spouse, children, community, work, etc. What about those commitments do you want to be included in your eighty-nine-year Mountain? For example, "At eighty-nine, I want to still be in love with my wife, have my kids in a healthy relationship with us, and continue the work that is my passion."

Now let's turn to the other Mountains, those benchmarks leading up to eight nine. Before we process through the rest of the Mountains, take a moment, and think about the things you've always dreamed of doing. Have you wanted to write a book, perform before an audience, write music, create art, travel to somewhere you've never been, or take a class? What dreams do you have that if left unfulfilled will make your life incomplete? Put those dreams in your timeline. For example, I wanted to record a CD before I was fifty years old, and I did! It went on my timeline, and I made it happen because I didn't let go of that dream.

Another helpful tool in looking at your timeline is to think about unchangeable life moments. Think about the age of your parents and an age range when you might be without them. This is a significant time in your life, and it is helpful to see that in the timeline. Of course, we can't predict death, but we can be aware of the range of when it will probably happen and see that time in our lives as a time of extended grief. (I usually tell clients to plan on a year of grief when their parents pass—something that is very helpful to know about in your timeline.)

Think also about when you will be empty nesters. One day you will wake up, and it will be just you and your spouse. What will that be like? Put that in your timeline and begin to prepare for it now. By that I mean you include in your timeline spending quality vacation time with your spouse so you do not become strangers when the kids depart the nest. Vacation time without the kids is of strategic importance for you, your marriage, and your children. Book it!

Here is a sample set of mountains for a thirty-five-year-old with two children ages six and four and parents who are sixty years old.

85-Year Mountain
- *Still in love with my spouse,*
- *Have a great relationship with my kids and grandkids, and*
- *Still doing significant work*

80-Year Mountain
- *Still in love with my spouse,*
- *Have a great relationship with my kids and grandkids,*
- *Still doing significant work but with less time, and*
- *Sell the house*

75-Year Mountain
- *Still in love with my spouse,*
- *Have a great relationship with my kids and grandkids,*
- *Still doing significant work,*
- *Sell the business, and*
- *Spend a year in France*

70-Year Mountain
- *Still in love with my spouse,*
- *Have a great relationship with my kids and grandkids,*
- *Still doing significant work, and*
- *Continue mentoring replacement at work*

65-Year Mountain
- *Still in love with my spouse,*
- *Have a great relationship with my kids and grandkids,*
- *Still doing significant work,*
- *Mentor replacement at work, and*
- *Grieving loss of parents*

60-Year Mountain
- *Still in love with my spouse,*
- *Have a great relationship with my kids and grandkids,*
- *Still doing significant work,*
- *Identify someone to take my place at work, and*
- *Write a book*

55-Year Mountain
- *Still in love with my spouse,*
- *Have a great relationship with my kids and grandkids, and*
- *Still doing significant work*

50-Year Mountain
- *Still in love with my spouse,*
- *Have a great relationship with my kids and grandkids,*
- *Still doing significant work,*
- *Has become an empty nester, and*
- *Travel*

45-Year Mountain
- *Still in love with my spouse*
  - *extended yearly vacation with my spouse,*
- *Have a great relationship with my kids and grandkids,*
- *Still doing significant work, and*
- *Investing in my kids' lives*

40-Year Mountain
- *Still in love with my spouse*
  - *extended yearly vacation with my spouse,*
- *Have a great relationship with my kids,*
- *Investing in my kids' lives,*
- *Start my own business, and*
- *Still doing significant work*

After sketching the basics of your eighty-nine-year Mountain and filling in some of the things mentioned above, we can begin to ask what you will be doing when you are seventy years old. The same process is involved, but you may have more clarity than you did for your eighty-nine-year Mountain.

Next is your sixty-five-year Mountain, the time of life when you probably expected to retire (before you read this book). At sixty-five, most of your friends will have retired and will be looking for something significant to do with their days. You, however, will be engaged in significant work that aligns with your eighty-nine-year Mountain and with your Star.

You can see slightly more of this sixty-five-year Mountain

than you can your eighty-nine-year Mountain or your seventy-year Mountain. Your view is still hazy though, and you can't see very much. That's OK too. You know you're going to climb this Mountain, and you're training even now for this climb. You can see more of this Mountain than the previous Mountains, and you should start to think about the equipment you will need to make this climb.

After thinking through the sixty-five-year Mountain, you should give some thought to the Mountain that is your life at fifty-five years old. The same issues will be involved here, and you should think about what you need to be accomplishing at this point in your life that will keep you on a pace to reach your sixty-five-year Mountain and your eighty-nine-year Mountain.

Most of the people I work with are looking for a certain degree of financial stability by age fifty-five, and this may be a benchmark for you also. Other benchmarks may be the extent to which your career will be established, the significance of the work you will have created, or the impact you will have had on the world at this point in your life. List these benchmarks underneath the Mountain you are describing.

Depending on your age from the fifty-five-year Mountain, you can look closer in and see the forty-five-year Mountain. This Mountain is clearer than the others are. You can see where the tree line ends and the snow begins. You can make out a pass that runs down the side of the Mountain, and you can see a road carved into the Mountain. This is similar to your life plan. You can see with more clarity some of the things that will be in your life at age forty-five. If you have children, they will be older. If you don't have children or aren't married, then you might consider the role these events could have in your life by the time you are forty-five.

You might also look at your life and think about what professional accomplishments you want to have achieved at this juncture. Again, it is helpful to list these various factors under the Mountain you are now describing.

At forty-five, your job will have more responsibilities, your parents will be older, and you will be running a little more slowly than you are now. You can probably put together a reasonably accurate picture of what your life might look like at this age. What are the goals and accomplishments you would like to obtain by then? Is more education required? Will you need to have start-up capital saved or raised by then? Will you need to relocate? What skills, experiences, and resources will you need in order to accomplish your goals?

Before we progress any further in describing the path toward the Mountain range, it might be helpful to look again at that picture in Colorado. As you gaze at the road leading into the mountains, you will notice that it tends to zigzag upward rather than go straight up. This will probably accurately describe your actual path of ascent. You won't be able to maintain a perfectly straight path to the top of the Mountains you create. Rather you will be forced to zigzag your way to the top. This means you may have to take some side steps that don't look like they are moving you immediately in the direction of the Mountain, but they are essential in ascending at a reasonable rate up the Mountain. A gradual climb in zigzag fashion is better than no climb at all. The good news will be that you are at least on your way up the right Mountain in your life.

If you're not yet thirty-five, continue to work backward with your life plan. With the forty-five-year Mountain in sight, you can see with even greater clarity your thirty-five-year Mountain. The thirty-five-year Mountain will creep up on you quickly. Just think back five years to where you were then and what has happened since. If you have children, think back to where they were and what they were doing five years ago, and you will probably be amazed at how quickly the time has gone by.

For your thirty-five-year Mountain, you will need to think about the specifics of where you want to be. Where do you want to live, and what do you want to be doing? What will you need to do to keep you on the path toward climbing your eighty-nine-year

Mountain? What resources will you need? What does the picture of your life look like in five years? Who are your friends? Where are your family members in their life journey, and where will they be in five years? What will you need to be doing in five years to prepare yourself to climb the forty-five-year Mountain?

Now we must look at the immediate Mountain—the two- to three-year Mountain. In the next two to three years, you will need to be doing specific things that will get you on your way to climbing this first Mountain—the Mountain that is five years away. If you have thought about your first Mountain and how quickly the last five years have passed, then you realize that two to three years fly by like a speeding train.

Although this time frame is so short that it is almost difficult to imagine any real changes happening, significant changes *can* take place in two to three years. You need to think about what you want to have in place in the next two to three years that will enable you to climb your first Mountain.

Think of the time between now and five years as preparation time for climbing the Mountains. These years are the foothills of the journey. You must climb them first before you can tackle the other Mountains. These foothills will prepare you for your journey, and they will give you valuable experience in climbing the higher, steeper Mountains that lie ahead.

In order to climb these foothills and the rest of the Mountains looming before you, you'll need to think about preparing yourself for the climb. What resources will you need for this great adventure? What will be in your backpack? What educational requirements will help you on the journey? What experiences will assist you in making the climb? What financial resources will be required? What personal contacts will you need?

Most of us thought that going to college or getting an advanced degree would provide us with enough preparation for our personal and professional climb. We thought we would earn an appropriate degree and then build a résumé that would enable us to climb the

Mountain of life. Later in life, we realize that the degree and résumé may be insufficient for us to climb the personal Mountains that our *Core Motivator* and Star have set before us.

After reading this book, you should know that a résumé only helps with a plot-driven life. You may have to prepare differently for a character-driven life, so now you may need to reassess your place on the path. Are you ready to begin the climb? Do you have all the resources you will need? What will it take to acquire the necessary resources you don't have?

Maybe you're forty years old, and your Mountains are going to require some additional education, but you can't imagine going back to school! When you realize, however, that you'll live to be eighty-nine years old and you are only halfway there now, a two-year investment in further education could be worthwhile.

Or perhaps one of your Mountains is to own your own business. If so, you realize that you need to reprioritize your spending so that you can save enough initial capital to begin the climb. Now is the best time to begin because it won't get any easier as time passes, and your life goes on.

Or perhaps you realize that you live in the wrong location for the kind of work you believe you're equipped for. You may not be able to move today, but you can begin thinking about when and how you'll make that move. We have all heard it said, "A journey of a thousand miles begins with a single step." Now you must define those first steps and plan how to begin.

START It!

Now that you understand the need to set out for the Mountains, it is time to discuss the specifics of determining your Mountains. I have saved this discussion until now because I want to be sure that you understand the kinds of goals you will be setting and the reasons behind those goals.

The acronym START will help you give form and shape to your Mountains.

S is for *Star*. Ask this question with everything you do, "Does this get me to my Star?" Will this step take you further in the direction of your Star, or are you walking in place, going backward, or wandering off the path? Perhaps the greatest advantage of beginning with your Star will be your ability to say no to certain things. By looking at your Star, you can ask the question, "Does this align with my Star?" If the answer is no, then you can reject whatever you're considering.

T is for *task*. What is the task? Can the goal be defined as a specific task, or is it so nebulous that you can't define it? In what tangible way will you know when you've completed this goal? How will you know if you have been successful in reaching this goal?

A is for *attainable*. Is completing this task or climbing this Mountain attainable? Is this Mountain climbable? If the strongest climber cannot complete the task, then you know it's not worth pursuing.

R is for *realistic*. Is climbing this Mountain or completing this task realistic? Can you really accomplish this? This is the time for a reality check. If there is no way you can climb this Mountain, then it's a bad Mountain for you. This question is the personal side of attainable. A task may be attainable for some people, but is it realistic to think *you* can accomplish it? If not, then you must reject the task.

T is for *timely*. What is the appropriate timetable for this Mountain? Does your five-year Mountain really take five years, or is it better to make this a seven-year goal or perhaps a two-year goal? What are the right time frames for each step along the path for each Mountain you are going to climb?

As you set each Mountain and follow the specific steps required to climb it, you can START it and assess whether or not you are moving in the right direction and climbing the right mountain. Once you have determined that you have good goals and have set realistic steps for accomplishing them, then you are ready to begin. You can take the first step.

What will you do today?

Success Doesn't Make You Successful

A last word about defining your Mountains: Remember that success (the achievement or acquisition of a goal or object you desire) doesn't necessarily make you successful. No manner of outward achievement changes the essence of who you are. A healthy way to view achievements, therefore, is to view them as the outward expression of who you are and of what truly matters to you. *Vision for Your Life* helps you identify the Mountains (benchmarks) that are *right for you*. The right Mountains are those that reflect your *Core Motivator* as well as your interests, desires, passion, and talents.

Aaron

Aaron is someone who changed his picture of the right Mountains for him as a result of the *Vision for Your Life* process. He is outgoing, good with people, and able to come up with insights that help others. However, both in business and in his volunteer work, he found that he struggled in holding formal positions of leadership. He became distant, reserved, and frustrated. As a result, he wasn't very effective.

When Aaron discovered that his *Core Motivator* was *Connecting*, he then realized that holding a formal leadership role made him feel disconnected from the people he was supposed to be leading. Leadership is lonely and the lack of connection left him very frustrated. At first, the solution seemed simple. Aaron needed to make an effort to connect with his team members. Then he would feel connected to them, and this would free him up to be a successful leader.

As we talked, however, it became evident that there was more to it than this. Aaron really didn't want a formal leadership position.

He preferred to work independently as a free agent. His picture of success was starting a business with his best friend and developing additional business relationships with other friends and associates with whom he also had a high level of connection, and whom he trusted from a business perspective. He didn't want any job working for someone else, and Aaron's real challenge was overcoming his fear that he couldn't succeed financially on his own. His picture of success had been a function of his fear that he couldn't have what he really wanted.

For Aaron, incorrectly defining success made it very difficult to sustain his motivation level. Even though he knew his *Core Motivator*, it was almost impossible to live out of it when he continued to cling to the wrong picture of success.

The great theologian Dietrich Bonhoeffer once told a student who was going to work for the Nazi-controlled German church, "There is no sense getting on a train going in the wrong direction just so you can walk opposite down the aisle."

When we live our lives in a direction that is not congruent with our STAR statement, it is like getting on the wrong train. It is going someplace you don't want to be, and you are running down the aisle in the opposite direction.

Aaron needed to get clear about where he ultimately wanted to be and to begin working toward that (more accurate) picture. Then living out of *Connecting*—his *Core Motivator*—would be much easier.

When Aaron was finally able to articulate his picture of being a free agent—sharing an office with his best friend, doing work that really mattered to him, and having the freedom to work with multiple clients in different geographic areas—he came alive. This picture was one that he would have no problem getting motivated to achieve.

Aaron's lesson holds true for the rest of us. When we allow our fears to define our picture of success and strive to achieve a picture we don't really want, then it is no wonder we can't get more motivated. When what we really want leads us to and reinforces our pictures of success, we eliminate many of the motivational obstacles that inhibit us. Practical obstacles remain. Aaron has a lot of hard work ahead of him to develop his own business, but the obstacles within Aaron that kept him on the wrong train were identified. After that, every inch of progress he made was an inch in the right direction.

Chapter 14

THINKING IN PICTURES

A picture is worth a thousand words.

Christmas is a big deal in our home. I can remember my wife shopping for Christmas decorations when we were dating—in July. We spent many Christmases at my parents' home with my extended family, flying there on Christmas Eve or Christmas Day.

One year while we were doing our usual Christmas Eve packing, I noticed my wife coming in from the grocery store with some fresh fruit. Since we were leaving the next morning, I thought that was odd, so I asked her about the fruit. She hesitated a bit and then mumbled something about having fondue with the boys after church that evening.

After hearing those bits and pieces of her mumbling, I said, "You have a picture of what you want this evening to look like, so why don't you let me know what it is and we can work together to make it happen."

She agreed to share her picture with me and let me help her achieve the picture of all of us going to church together and then sitting in our den with the Christmas tree lit with the fire going and enjoying fondue while watching videos of our boys' early Christmases. It was a great picture, and I was more than happy to assist her in making it happen.

I then went up to the boys' rooms and told them their mother had a picture of what she wanted to happen that evening, that I agreed with her, and that if they had other plans for the evening, they needed to change them. The result was that we had a wonderful evening of being together and enjoying the fondue and videos. After about an hour, the boys gave me the look that said, "Dad, please save us." I turned to my wife and said, "How are we doing? Has this been a good version of your picture?" She was thrilled that it had lasted that long, and everyone was happy. She said thank you to the boys, and they went to their rooms. She and I smiled at each other, enjoyed a little more fondue, and reminisced about the days when the boys were much younger.

Most of us think in pictures. When we talk about vision, we are talking about the picture we see. When I speak of a *Vision for Your Life*, I'm talking about how you see a picture of what your life could be like. Most of us have some kind of picture of what we want our lives to be like, and we're working to make that picture happen. We have pictures of what our work should look like, what our homes should look like, what our relationships should be, and the way our lives should grow and develop. In fact, we tend to think in pictures all the time even though we rarely articulate our picture(s).

One example is our picture of family. Many husbands and wives have conflicts over their different views about raising children. Many times, the husband and wife have different pictures in their minds of what it means to be a parent. The father has built a picture based on his background and experiences, and the mother has developed her own picture based on her own background and experiences. They may find themselves in conflict over a specific aspect of parenting. One helpful communication tool is for each parent to describe to the other, in as much detail as possible, his or her own picture. Then the couple can begin to work together to resolve the conflicts that arise from the combination of their pictures.

The same is true in every other aspect of our lives. In our work or volunteer activities, we have a picture of how we think things should go, and we are working toward that picture. Successful teams work together toward the same picture of success and when there are different pictures the result is conflict, hurt, and failure.

This idea of thinking in pictures will be helpful in this *visioneering* process also. For most of us, this exercise will not be as much an exercise of developing a new vision as it is one of revision. Most of us already have a vision—or picture—of our lives, but in this process, we are going to create a revision as well as create some new pictures of what our lives will look like.

In the introduction to this book, I briefly mentioned the idea of thinking in pictures. At this point in the process, thinking in pictures is important because you will see your life in the various pictures your mind paints.

An artist paints what he sees in his mind's eye. When Monet painted water lilies, he painted what he saw when he looked at the water lilies in his garden. What Monet saw was different from what the average eye would see. After he painted his impression of those water lilies on canvas, the rest of us could view the beauty Claude Monet had seen. This is the work of the artist, to create for others what the artist sees, hears, or feels in his own mind or soul. Some artists transfer images from their minds onto canvas, paper, or film. Still others do it with music or photographs, but the core function of the artist is the same—to create a work for others to enjoy that once existed only in the mind or soul of the artist.

In describing the Mountains of your life, you're going to be painting with your mind.

Now that you have established your *Core Motivator*, set your *Star*, plotted a *life path*, and defined *Mountains*, it's time to look at an overview of the whole picture. So once again, let's ask the question, "What will your life look like every day when you are living this vision?" Can you paint a word picture of your life that will be an icon or a kind of snapshot that would tell the whole story of your life? Your picture should include three key elements. First your picture should be of a specific place with color and vibrancy. It should be someplace that you can see clearly in your mind's eye.

Second your picture must include your Star statement. The picture must be a summation of what you want your whole life to be about, which you have captured in your Star statement.

Third your picture should include action. This picture is not a still life; it is a vibrant, clear, and active snapshot of you engaged in your Star.

For example, my picture is of a house in France where my friends come to visit and have significant conversations. My *Core Motivator* is *Connecting*. I can give you very specific details about this picture. I can describe the house, the patio, and the conversation. But the picture doesn't have to be in France—that just happens to be my favorite place—so I make it my picture. The *Connecting* elements— friends and significant conversation—are what illuminate the picture for me.

When faced with a new job opportunity or a decision to make about life, I can look at this picture and ask the question, "Does this activity get me to my house in France?" In other words, when faced with different options, I have a picture that is helpful in putting the various choices in perspective.

I have a friend who is a *Creating Core Motivator*. His picture is seat 1A. He sees himself on an airplane seated in first class on his way to creating a solution to someone's problem. He doesn't really like to fly, but the picture tells him what his vision is all about—creating solutions for the whole world.

EXERCISE NUMBER 10: DEVELOPING A WORD PICTURE

Take a few minutes now to write down your word picture. Add as many details to your picture as you can to make it really come alive. If possible, create an actual picture of yourself doing something in that scenario and place it in a prominent place as a reminder of what you really want your life to be about.

My picture is my screen saver. Every day I think about what I want my life to be about, and I ask myself the question, "Is what I'm doing today getting me to my picture?"

We need to remember that the good is the enemy of the best. Sometimes we choose the good because we haven't defined the best. When we get a vision for our lives based on our *Core Motivator*, we have defined the best. We can now use the picture of that life path to help us make good decisions for staying on the path.

Chapter 15

CHANGE IS DIFFICULT

People resist change.
—Paul Kooistra

M Y friend, Dr. Paul Kooistra, says that one of the indisputable laws of psychology is that people resist change. Change is difficult. It is far easier for us to continue along the path we are already on than to change paths.

We know that change disrupts the normal patterns of our lives. Choosing to set a new direction for our lives may require painful sacrifices for our families and for us. It may require us to change jobs or perhaps even relocate to a different city. We may have to move away from our extended family—or it may mean moving closer to family! It could mean living where we don't like the weather or taking a job where we will be at the bottom of the ladder again. We might have to go back to school or serve as an apprentice.

While it is true that change is difficult and we all resist change in our lives, it is also true that staying the same can be more painful than changing. When the pain level of remaining where we are becomes higher than the perceived pain of the change, then we are ready to change.

The *Vision-for-Your-Life* process shows us that any pain associated with change is worthwhile when we focus on who we truly are—our *Core Motivator*.

You won't be doing an *extreme makeover* of who you are, and you probably won't be retooling your entire skill set. Most of us are already working in fields that are closely aligned with our gifts and abilities. The truly significant change will be in the way you exercise your particular gifts and abilities. The changes in your life will occur when you live more fully out of your *Core Motivator* while using your gifts and skills. Real change takes place as you discover the potential God has in mind for who He created you to be because you will see more clearly your *Core Motivator* and know it is your greatest strength.

In my consulting practice, I've noticed that some people initially come to me wanting a quick fix to their immediate problem. They want problems that have taken years to develop to be erased in one easy step. Any of us who have faced the need to diet have wished for a magic pill that we could take at night, which would give us the perfect weight in the morning. That pill doesn't exist, and neither does a quick and easy solution to building a vision for your life.

When I began in youth ministry, my predecessor told me that the greatest challenge in the job would be to deal with parents who wanted me to fix in two months the problems that had taken fifteen years to create. Fixing those problems that fast is impossible, and so is quickly implementing long-term changes in the direction of your life. Over the long haul, however, real change can occur.

You can begin by finding success in the small steps. What one thing will you do today that will emphasize living out of your *Core Motivator*? Is there a decision you can make that will be different if you make it out of *who you really are* instead of the false you?

Here are some possible first steps for the various *Core Motivators*:

1. *Connecting.* Schedule a couple of one-on-one meetings with no other agenda than connecting.

2. *Belonging.* Find a group or gather some friends and measure your level of enjoyment from simply being together.

3. *Caring.* Look at the people in your life and ask which ones are particularly needy. Then find a way to care *for* them without trying to take care *of* them.

4. *Serving.* Look at the people in your life and choose one to serve today.

5. *Giving.* Sort out the various philanthropic requests you receive and make a significant gift to a cause especially close to you.

6. *Creating.* Look at the projects you are involved in and decide on one where you can focus your energy.

7. *Perfecting.* Look at the various projects in your life that frustrate you because they are not perfect. Choose one to either release or work to make perfect.

These represent the first steps, and as you work on these actions analyze your own emotional journey. Are you energized by living out of your *Core Motivator?* Or are you drawn into the negative side of your *Core Motivator?*

What do you need to say no to because it is the negative representation of your *Core Motivator?*

For some people, a journal is helpful. Start a daily journal and record the instances where you saw yourself initiating out of the strength of your *Core Motivator.* Also note those times when you backed away from being fully you because of your fears. As you record each day, also look back on previous days to identify patterns and try to change that behavior the next time a similar situation arises.

As you journal, notice the small victories and the gradual changes that indicate you are beginning to better navigate your path.

NAVIGATE

The key to living out of your *Core Motivator* is to navigate your daily life. Every day you make scores of decisions; in making those decisions, you navigate the path of your life. The key to living a full life out of who you really are lies in navigating it well. As you become more self-aware of the decisions you are making and why you are making them, you'll be able to make better decisions that are more congruent with who you are.

As I mentioned at the beginning of this chapter, change is difficult, and we all resist change. As you reflect on where your life has been and where you want it to go, have the courage to face the necessary steps that lead to change. Then go with courage, knowing that God, who created you, will not abandon His workmanship.

Chapter 16

APPLICATIONS

One life, one Day-Timer.
—Charles R. Hobbs

R emember the story about the Hobbs seminar (chapter 5)? Hobbs's premise is that we are to view our lives as a unified whole. While each person's life has component parts, your life should be guided by *one* vision. As I presented the idea of *Core Motivators*, I discovered that these concepts apply to every area of our lives.

In this chapter, we will discuss the application of our *Core Motivator* in three specific areas of life: business, family, and faith.

BUSINESS

A senior leader supervises a team of salespeople and runs one of the most successful divisions in his organization. Employee 1 is a member of the team who comes to the leader's office every day, just to talk. He sits in the chair close to his boss's desk to ask about his day or to share something about his own day. The length of their conversation varies depending on the day, and the topics can encompass work, sports, family, or other relationships. The leader has become accustomed to these visits and looks forward to

Employee 1 dropping in. The leader thinks that Employee 1 is the best employee he has ever had on his team.

Another employee also comes into the leader's office a couple of times a week. He doesn't have much to say, except that the team should get together more often. The leader views the second employee as an annoyance and doesn't understand why he wants to have more team meetings. Unlike his meetings with Employee 1, the leader dreads Employee 2's office visits.

When the leader evaluates his employees, his own *Core Motivator* colors his view of each person's performance. Since he and Employee 1 share the same *Core Motivator—Connecting*—the leader gives Employee 1 a positive evaluation. Employee 2's *Core Motivator* of *Belonging* causes the leader angst; therefore, he rates Employee 2's performance as low. In this case, the leader has just evaluated two members of his team not on their actual performance but on the employee's compatibility with the leader's *Core Motivator* of *Connecting*.

This same principle is true in every area of our lives. We tend to appreciate and value those who share our *Core Motivators* and undervalue those with different *Core Motivators*. In business, we tend to elevate those whose *Core Motivators* match our own.

I once had a man call me and ask for advice on hiring a salesperson. He was very excited about a particular candidate but had some minor concerns about the candidate's résumé. In fact, nothing in the résumé indicated this person would be good at sales. A particular assessment tool we were using even showed he would probably struggle in a sales role.

The man on the phone was a *Connecting Core Motivator* and had great chemistry with the candidate. He had connected with this guy and was ready to hire him on the basis of that connection alone— even in the face of other data suggesting he would be a bad hire.

We tend to think that if someone is like us, they must be worth hiring or promoting. It can be subconscious and unintentional, but it is a real behavior that we need to be aware of. When I pointed out to my friend that he saw himself in this potential new hire and was blinded to the deficiencies of the guy's resume, he was shocked but knew I was right and did not hire the guy.

The healthiest teams will have a diversity of *Core Motivators*, and the successful leader will value and appreciate each person for who he or she is. Different *Core Motivators* bring different perspectives to the team. When we understand the various *Core Motivators* on a team, we can better align people with the best position for them.

A boss with a *Connecting Core Motivator*, as in the previous example, needs someone on his team who is able to see potential candidates for their abilities without the bias of compatibility in connecting.

Belonging Core Motivators will see the team as a whole and will have the perspective of building camaraderie within the team. These people are good corporate team players who are a kind of glue that holds a team together.

Caring Core Motivators will see the needs of the various team members and know when someone is hurting.

Serving Core Motivators will be the first to jump in and take on a task to help the team.

Giving Core Motivators will willingly sacrifice for the team.

Creating Core Motivators will constantly think of what the team can create next.

Perfecting Core Motivators will look at what the team produces and seek to make it perfect.

Diversity within a team can be helpful once we understand people's *Core Motivators* and can speak their language.

Larry

Larry supervises a large staff covering ten states and reports directly to the president of the company. During a conference call in which the president was announcing a new initiative, David (one of Larry's direct reports) challenged the president on numerous points of the new project. Larry not only was embarrassed by David's inappropriate behavior, but he was also frustrated by David's constant challenging of everything going on in the organization. Larry is a *Caring Core Motivator* and doesn't understand why David would act this way, and he asked me for some help in working with him.

I explained to Larry that David is a *Perfecting Core Motivator* and therefore sees everything through the lens of how it could be perfect. He wasn't trying to be belligerent; he just needed to see the total picture of how it could be perfect. Larry saw the situation through his lens of *Caring* and was hurting for the president while David saw the situation through his lens of perfecting and wanted to know how this was going to be done perfectly.

My suggestion to Larry was to prepare David beforehand. He could tell David that not all the details of the perfect picture would ever be given during an initial conversation but that after the call, he would be glad to work on the picture with him. Larry needed to understand that what appeared to be criticism wasn't really a criticism but was David's need to have the perfect picture painted for him. David needed to understand that nothing is ever perfect, and there is a time and a place to ask the appropriate questions to the president.

How many good people have been lost to an organization because the supervisor and the employee weren't able to speak the same *Core Motivator* language?

FAMILY

I got a call one day from an acquaintance named Mark who heard me speak at a conference. He said, "Bob, I'd like to go through *Vision for Your Life*."

Because this kind of call hardly ever happens, I am usually suspicious of them when they do. I said to him, "Mark, I'd be glad to work with you, but I don't do marriage counseling." I don't even know why I said that. It just came to my mind, and I did.

There was a long silence on the other end of the phone. I finally said, "Mark, why don't you tell me what's going on?"

He said, "I've had an affair, and I've just told my wife, who is sitting here next to me, and I didn't know who else to call."

I talked to both of them for a while and told him that I would be thrilled to work with him after they got some counseling. Mark and his wife did get some good counseling, and several months later, I met with him to go through *Vision for your life*. The counseling had been good for them, and they had worked on some of their issues. Now it was time for Mark to figure out who he was and what really motivated him.

Mark's *Core Motivator* is *Caring*, and he is attracted to needy people. His wife isn't needy in a way that Mark can take care of her, so when he met someone at work who was needy and whom he could take care of, he found himself involved with her instead of his wife.

For Mark, the key has been to navigate his relationships out of understanding his *Core Motivator*. This means that while he recognizes his attraction to needy people, he also realizes that there are appropriate ways to care for them and lines that cannot be crossed. It means that while his wife may not be as outwardly needy as he would like, she also has her needs, and he must see the ways in which he can care for her.

When we look at the dynamics of a family, we see that the different *Core Motivators* of the couple determine different paradigms for the way the family unit is to be conducted.

For example, if the *Core Motivator* of one person is *Serving* and the *Core Motivator* of the other is *Creating*, they may clash over the way they interact with their friends, their extended families, and their children. The *Serving* person will want to look for opportunities to serve his or her friends. The *Creating* person will want to look for new things to do and will become easily bored by repeating the same activity many times.

The two of them need to learn to find a commonality in creating new ways to serve people. That is a simplistic example, but let's turn to a more difficult problem.

Barb's *Core Motivator* is *Belonging.* She has a wonderful son who is sociable but also content to play by himself. She was visiting a friend who had two boys of her own, and the three boys played together for a while. After a time, her son was content to play alone.

Barb was panic-stricken. She was seeing her son through her own *Core Motivator* of *Belonging* and was frightened that he wouldn't fit in with groups of other kids. In reality, her son is social and quite capable of playing with other kids, but he is also independent enough to choose whether he wants to play with others or not. He is content to play by himself, and it is evident at an early stage that *Belonging* is not his *Core Motivator.*

Barb's challenge is to affirm him for who he is and to encourage him to live his life through his own *Core Motivator* (whatever that may be) and experience all of his life to its fullest.

As parents, we need to look for our children's *Core Motivators* and be careful we are not projecting our own *Core Motivators* on them or expecting them to be like us.

Another example might be a *Connecting Core Motivator,* whose spouse doesn't understand them. They resent the others' friends, and when the *Connecting Core Motivator* spouse has breakfast with a friend, they might tell their spouse that the friend is in trouble and needs their counseling. They are running from their true self—their *Core Motivator*—because they don't want to cause a problem with their spouse.

Mary is a *Serving Core Motivator,* and she looks for ways to be involved in service projects in the community and at church. Her husband doesn't understand why she never has time for him. He resents both the church and the people she helps.

Jim is a *Creating Core Motivator* and is constantly looking for new projects to do around the house. His wife wants to settle into the house they have, but he is always looking for the next house to take on as a project.

Or let's consider a *Caring Core Motivator* who has filled their life with needy people. Their spouse might become tired of them spending all their time with hurting people and is frustrated by the needs of so many people that never seem to go away.

When we don't understand our spouse's *Core Motivator*, then we don't understand why our spouses do what they do or the way they do it. Instead of encouraging our spouses to be all that God created them to be, we become a discouragement to them because we want them to be someone other than who they truly are.

Let's look at the above examples again.

Although a spouse can love the fact that the other person is a *Connecting Core Motivator*, they may want all of their partner's relationships to be with the family because they are a *Belonging Core Motivator*, and the family is their team.

Mary's husband loves that she is a *Serving Core Motivator*; however, he wants her to serve *him*.

Jim's wife loves what he creates. She is a *Connecting Core Motivator* and wants him to create a wonderful place where she can entertain her friends.

A *Caring Core Motivator's* husband might be originally attracted to them because of their caring heart. But if he is a *Perfecting Core Motivator* and has become increasingly troubled by all the imperfect people around their house who never seem to get better, he might become very frustrated.

A successful marriage requires both people to appreciate the uniqueness of the person they married. It also requires each person to understand the negative side of his or her *Core Motivator* and be sensitive to the needs of the other person.

Connecting Core Motivators need relationships outside of the family but not at the expense of their family. Spouses must learn to appreciate the balancing act that must be maintained between connecting with family and connecting with others.

Mary needs to see that there are avenues of serving right in her own home and that some of the outside opportunities to serve can become all-consuming if she lets them. She needs to be wise in deciding how to allocate her time in the various places she serves so that her husband won't feel neglected.

Jim needs to see that many opportunities to create exist outside of fixing his own house. His wife needs to affirm some of his outside creating and see that when he is engaged deeply in a project of creating, he is trying to become the person God made him to be.

Caring Core Motivators must see that they are attracted to needy people, and the imbalance of those people in their lives can be unhealthy for them. No one is perfect, and the spouses of *Caring Core Motivators* must recognize that everyone has issues, but at the same time, their spouse doesn't need to turn their home into a clinic.

The point is that we must learn not only to respect but also to affirm the person God created our spouse to be while at the same time working together to bring balance into our mutual lives.

THE CHRISTIAN FAITH

We even see the Christian faith through our own *Core Motivator*. We view the Gospel through the lens of our own *Core Motivator* and tend to believe that ours is the *true* meaning of the faith. Here are some examples of how this works itself out.

Connecting Core Motivators see the faith as a relationship with God or with Christ. These are the people who are focused on their personal spiritual experience and who see evangelism as a relational activity.

Belonging Core Motivators see the faith as being about their community. They are focused on forming small groups at a church and believe that outsiders will be drawn to the faith by seeing and experiencing the community of believers.

Caring Core Motivators see faith as how they care for one another and those in need. They are focused on forming care groups and taking care of those in need. They believe that evangelism happens when they take care of the needy.

Serving Core Motivators see faith as an expression of how they serve one another. They focus on servant leadership and are concerned about acts of service. They believe that evangelism happens through mission trips or service projects.

Giving Core Motivators see faith as how they give of themselves, their time, talent, and treasure to others. These people are focused on what they can sacrificially give to each other and the church. They believe that evangelism happens when they give to those in need.

Creating Core Motivators see faith as anything they can create to expand the kingdom. They are focused on the new campaign, the new program, and the new building. They believe that evangelism happens by creating a new program or facility to spread the Gospel.

Perfecting Core Motivators see faith as how they are becoming perfect in their walk with Christ. These are the *holiness* people who are focused on our sanctification. They believe that evangelism happens when Christians model perfection to the world around them.

The body of Christ needs all the *Core Motivators* to function well. Only God—and Jesus as fully God and fully man—has all the *Core Motivators*. We are each a reflection of His nature, and we bear His image, but we do not possess all the *Core Motivators*. We need each other because only when we operate as a body can we truly function as a church.

Let's look at an example of how the various *Core Motivators* work in a church setting. Let's imagine the church is going to do a mission trip to build houses in South America.

The Caring Core Motivators ask, "Are there needy people? I'm in."

The Serving Core Motivators ask, "Do we get to serve someone? I'm in."

The Giving Core Motivators ask, "Why don't we just give them money? I'm out."

The Creating Core Motivators ask, "Will I get to build something? I'm in."

The Perfecting Core Motivators ask, "Will we be able to build a perfect house? Will I have to work with imperfect people? Maybe out, maybe in."

The Connecting Core Motivators ask, "Is anyone going on this trip that I will connect with? Maybe I'm in and maybe I'm out."

The Belonging Core Motivators ask, "Will I get to be part of the team? I'm in."

Well maybe all those responses aren't exact, but you can get a picture of how the dynamics play out. The point is that maybe not everyone should go on the mission trip. We need to ask what role each *Core Motivator* will play and design our outreach efforts to enable the whole team to exercise the most of who they are.

Maybe it's best if the *Connecting Core Motivators* don't go if they are going to spend the week depressed because they don't connect with anyone. Maybe the *Giving Core Motivators* should write a check and stay home. Maybe the *Perfecting Core Motivators* should stay home if they can't deal with imperfections in the project. Or maybe they all should go and be stretched out of their comfort zone. The individuals must decide for themselves, but they can decide with eyes wide open, knowing that this may be a place where God will use them.

A note on pastors: I have a tremendous amount of respect for and love for those in the full-time ministry, particularly those in the pastoral ministry. I believe they have one of the toughest jobs on the planet, and for the most part, they are undervalued and unappreciated. I have met with many pastors who have been sent to me as part of their severance package. It's not a fun time. They are angry, hurt, and confused. They have been faithful, loved God, and tried to serve their flock. The *Perfecting* and *Creating Core Motivators* have not sufficiently relationally engaged their members, boards, or elders, and they have been fired. The *Caring, Serving,* and *Giving Core Motivators* have met the needs of their people, but it seems that it is a short-lived dance. When the people figure out that the *Caring, Serving,* or *Giving Core Motivator* pastor doesn't know what to do with them when they're healthy, the pastor is gone. The *Connecting* and *Belonging Core Motivators* are great with the people but come into conflict with the members who want the church to grow. It is a sad state, and in each case, there is great freedom in understanding how they can go forward being the person God created them to be.

The difficult lesson is for the congregation and elders to understand that no one has all the *Core Motivators* and that we must work together and appreciate each other for what we each bring to the party. The pastors must understand their own *Core Motivators* and what they bring to the party in terms of their strengths and also their weaknesses. They need to learn to lead from their strengths and hire to their weakness, building a team that serves their congregation and reaches out to the world with the Gospel. This is the key to healthy churches that present a holistic view of the body of Christ to a world desperately in need of the Gospel.

Chapter 17

APPLYING THE PROCESS
TO ORGANIZATIONS

E very business is a people business, every problem is a people
problem, and every solution is a people solution.

Every organization is made up of people, and the people define
the organization. It is the people in an organization who hold it
together and make it grow. Understanding the people—who they
are and what their *Core Motivator* is—provides the key to building
a successful team and a successful organization.

In this chapter, we will look at the impact of understanding *Core
Motivators* on leaders, teams, and boards.

LEADERS

Leaders are responsible for establishing the vision for the
organization and putting together a group of followers who will
implement that vision. It is important to understand the *Core
Motivator* of the leader(s) of an organization so that both the leader
and his or her followers can understand where, why, and how they
are being led.

Each *Core Motivator* will lead out of who they are, their

individual *Core Motivator*. The *Connecting Core Motivator* will lead out of relationships, the *Belonging Core Motivator* will lead out of a sense of team building, etc. When we understand the *Core Motivator* of the leader of an organization, we can understand why they do what they do and the way they do it.

When members of a team understand the *Core Motivator* of the leader, they are able to better process how and why decisions are made and give context to the decisions.

The *Core Motivator* of the leader(s) will also affect the core values of the organization. For example, let's look at an organization that has customer satisfaction as one of its core values. The previous CEO was a *Serving Core Motivator* and believed that service was the key to success. The existing management team developed an approach of serving to meet that core value. Next let's say that the management team changes. A new CEO is brought in whose *Core Motivator* is *Connecting*.

This new CEO may still hold to the ideals of customer satisfaction, but he will also want to drive the company to emphasize relationships with customers over other priorities. This will result in a different approach to customer satisfaction than that of the previous management team. They will continue to serve the customers, but the driving force behind what they do will be connecting with clients. This will result in a very different environment for the company—and for the customers.

TEAMS

As noted previously, it is important for team members to understand the *Core Motivator* of the leader, but it is also important for them to understand the *Core Motivator* of the other members of the team.

Additionally, when a leader understands the *Core Motivators* of the people on his or her team, he or she is better able to supervise them. Supervision becomes an exercise in helping people meet the objectives of the organization's vision out of who they are and the part they play in accomplishing the vision.

In his book, *Good to Great*, Jim Collins talked about getting the right people on the bus and in the right seats. By understanding a person's *Core Motivator*, we can help discern if they are the right person in the right seat on the bus.

For example, if the job requires a high degree of perfection, then a *Perfecting Core Motivator* is best for that job. If the job requires a high degree of people engagement, then a *Connecting* or *Belonging Core Motivator* might be best for that job.

Teams should be built with the understanding of which *Core Motivator* is best suited for a particular job, and recruiting for that position should include a *Core Motivator* assessment.

When members of a team look around the table, they should know that the various members of the team see their job through the lens of their unique *Core Motivator* and appreciate what each member brings to the team.

Ted, Jim, and Pat

Ted's *Core Motivator* is *Perfecting*, and when he became partners with Jim and Pat, he thought he was bringing his ability to make their processes perfect. Jim's *Core Motivator* is *Caring*, and he looked at the partnership as a place to hire people and take care of them. Pat's *Core Motivator* is *Creating*, and he invented a new process that would make the three of them millionaires.

At first, there was so much work to do that everyone was totally engaged in getting the business off the ground. After a couple of years, however, relationships started to deteriorate between the partners. Ted didn't want to hire any more needy people—he was striving for perfection. Pat thought people were a resource that could be added or subtracted from the company as the needs of the company demanded, and he saw no need to treat the employees as anything other than a resource. Jim was getting tired of his two partners whom he viewed as cold and heartless. He wanted to hire more people he could take care of.

Rather than appreciate what each partner brought to the company, they resented and blamed each other when things didn't go well. When these conflicts finally blew up at a board meeting, it was too late to undo some of the damage that had been done to the partnership.

BOARDS

In large corporations, a different dynamic exists because the ownership of the organization is more widespread and diverse. Many times, you are dealing with a board of directors and stockholders. Nonetheless, the stockholders and board hire a management team to run the organization. Thus, the various *Core Motivators* of the board and management team will influence the decisions made for the organization as a whole. Most notably, the *Core Motivators* of the board will be reflected in whom they hire as CEO and how they evaluate success.

The *Core Motivators* of key individuals in an organization are always and inevitably reflected in an organization's mission statement and in the way the organization is run. It may not be immediately obvious, but the personal *Core Motivators* and goals of key stakeholders are at work in the background, driving many decisions. The *Core Motivators* may not be obvious, but they are present and at work in guiding the organization. When no one knows what those *Core Motivators* are, there is misunderstanding and conflict because the *Core Motivators* of the various individuals see the world through their different *Core Motivator* lenses.

This may be the reason why so many organizations get bogged down in company politics and turf battles that are counter-productive and detrimental to the health of the organization. Different people in leadership positions see the world through the different lenses of their *Core Motivators* and can't understand why everyone else doesn't see the world the way they do.

For example, if a person with a *Creating Core Motivator* dominates a board of directors, then that person may drive the organization to hire a CEO with the same *Creating Core Motivator*. The new CEO will build a management team that reflects his or her *Core Motivator* of *Creating*, and those with different *Core Motivators* will resist the change.

This new management team will be well received by the board because it sees the CEO as strengthening the team. When others in the organization begin to ask questions like "Where is our compassion?" or "What happened to our service?" then the potential for conflict is aroused and the political infighting begins.

The danger here is that an organization becomes heavily weighted on the *Core Motivator* of the leader(s) without appreciating the need to develop a team that reflects all seven of the *Core Motivators*.

Good teams value what each *Core Motivator* can bring to the party—what each *Core Motivator* sees. However, if the leadership of a team does not understand the various *Core Motivators*, then it is impossible for them to build the highly functional team that is required for success.

When leaders understand the various *Core Motivators* of the people on their team, then they are able to understand how each team member sees the world, why they react to certain circumstances the way they do, and how they approach their various responsibilities. In other words, they are able to understand *why* each member of their team does *what* they do the *way* they do it.

SOLE PROPRIETORSHIPS AND PARTNERSHIPS

The *Core Motivators* of the key stakeholders have a lot more to do with vision and decision-making than we may know or want to admit. I believe that every organization reflects the *Core Motivator(s)* of the people leading the organization, the core values, and the vision statement, and the key decisions of an organization reflect the *Core Motivators* of the key stakeholders.

In the case of a sole proprietor or a partnership, the vision, values, and decisions will reflect the *Core Motivators* of the owner(s). The vision for the company will be closely suited to the vision of the sole proprietor or partners. Once they have defined the vision plan for their lives, then they can look at the vision for the business to make sure it fits congruently into the life vision of the individual(s).

In organizations with teams of owners or managers, it is important to understand the *Core Motivators* of the various stakeholders on the board and management team in order to understand the values, vision, and decision-making of those stakeholders.

By beginning the visioning process with the key individuals involved in an organization, fewer unmatched dreams will plague the organization down the road. How many political fights could have been avoided, and how many partnerships (and friendships) might have been saved if the individual visions and *Core Motivators* of the people involved were identified at the beginning of the partnership?

A Broken Pastor

As I sat in church, I noticed that everything about the place was a reflection of its pastor. The contemporary design of the building, the comfortable chairs, the stage, and the curtains—everything was a reflection of who the pastor was.

I knew this because I had the opportunity to be in the pastor's home once. It had been a large group setting in another town, and he was a gracious host. His house was a beautiful creation, just like his church. He had started the church more than ten years before my visit. He had grown the church into one of the biggest in the area; it was a model for the denomination.

As I sat in that church, I was also grieved because he had left the church, the ministry, and his wife. My guess is that one of two things occurred. One possibility is that he is a man with a *Creating Core Motivator* who was bored because he had finished creating the church. A second possibility is that he has another *Core Motivator* and was living out of his false self, so his true *Core Motivator* was starved.

I mention this example because it is also my observation that boards and managers can become enamored with the *Creating Core Motivators* and quickly promote and affirm them. When this happens, the organization becomes one-dimensional and shallow. When the organization becomes too weighted toward one *Core Motivator*, then it fails to see the world through the various lenses that are a reality of life.

His church and the denomination affirmed him for his creative efforts in building the church. But the whole body of Christ would have been better served if he had known his *Core Motivator*—known what actually drove him and how his longest suit was used to glorify God. He might have been able to see the pitfalls, knowing the potential for boredom and the need for new challenges. He might have been able to be faithful in his marriage and better navigated his need to create the next thing. He, his family, his church, and the community would have been better served if Mark had known himself better.

When Values Change

When the leadership of an organization changes, the values of that organization often change with the new person because the new person brings a different *Core Motivator* to the leadership role. When new people are added to or replace an existing team, they bring with them their own personal *Core Motivators*, and these become part of the new set of core values for the organization. Even when the core values of the organization remain the same (because they have been etched in the corporate stone), they become shaded with the different colors of the new member's *Core Motivators*. Individuals form core values—not the other way around.

A More Engaged Workforce

In addition to the corporate dynamics listed above, the *Vision for Your Life* process is also beneficial to an organization because as individuals live their lives to the fullest, they are at their peak of productivity. Specifically, the *Vision for Your Life* process benefits both the individual and the organization in the following ways:

1. *by providing individual fulfillment for its employees;*
2. *by providing a catalyst for effective teamwork, and a common language for teams;*
3. *by retaining top employees as both the employer and employee have a common framework in which to discuss the deepest desires of the employee; and*
4. *by providing outplacement services to employees who no longer fit into the organization.*

Chapter 18

CONCLUSION

R ecently I had the opportunity to sit with some people who had been through the *Vision for Your Life* process. I got to listen to their reflections on how their lives had changed since going through the process. Person after person said that the greatest benefit is that they finally know who they are, and they are seeking to live out of their *Core Motivator* every day.

As we finish this discussion of *Building a Vision for Your Life*, the entire process can be summarized by one statement, "Know who you are and be it." The challenge for each of us, no matter what stage of life we're in, is to find the true person God created and to fully *be* that person.

One day I got a call from a former client who had been offered a great job with a Major League Baseball franchise. His *Core Motivator* is *serving*, and he asked me what he should do.

The first thing I said to him was "If you don't take the job, I will!" I was only kidding, but the thrill of working for a Major League Baseball franchise was very tempting for him and would be for me too.

My advice to my client was to sit down with the potential employer and tell him about the process he had just been through. I advised him to tell the employer that his *Core Motivator* was *Serving* and that if they wanted him in their organization, he would be thrilled to work with them. However, he would do the job out of his *Core Motivator*.

He took my advice and called me back a few days later. The baseball team had told him that they had just let the previous person in this position go because he wasn't a team player, and yes, they thought they would like to have him work for them. Of course, they would! Who wouldn't?

The very thing we all want is to interact with people who know who they are and are not trying to be someone else. We like to be around people who are free to be themselves and who will show us the path to living our lives with that kind of honesty. If we have the courage to look deep inside ourselves and see the core of the person God created and if we have the confidence to take that person into the world we live in, we will not only experience great personal freedom but also give others the courage to be their true selves.

You should know that there is also a downside to not identifying your *Core Motivator*. If you never find your *Core Motivator*, then you run the risk of never being fully yourself. You run the risk of being less than the person God made you to be. In this sense, you are missing out, and so are those around you.

You may even be slipping into the downward slide of career frustration, family conflict, depression, and a host of other maladies because you are afraid to be who God made you to be. You must face your fears, take the risk (there is, in fact, very little risk), and apply the reality of who you are to the life you are living.

It will be in the application of your being who you truly are— living it out every day – that you will experience the reality of God working in you. Therein lies the joy of being fully alive. It is the joy of being used by God to accomplish His purposes. This is the joy of being an instrument in the hand of God and experiencing Him using you to His glory. The challenge before us all is to have the courage to know who we are and to be it. And to return to Eric Liddle, when you are being fully you, you will feel His pleasure.

Working with a consultant through the *Vision for Your Life* process involves three sessions. During that time, we help you discover your *Core Motivator*, establish your Star, and set your personal Mountains. For more information about working through the *Vision for Your Life* process with a personal consultant or to order more copies of this book, please feel free to contact me using the information given.

About Bob Perkins

B ob Perkins is an executive coach, consultant, teacher, leader, husband, and father. He is a *Connecting Core Motivator* who at the age of forty redefined his life.

He spent twenty-two years in youth ministry and still looks back on those years working with high school kids as an incredible gift. His book, *No Banana Splits: A Perspective on Youth Ministry*, continues to be used as a training resource.

In 2003 he started Bob Perkins Consulting and enjoys "being in it" with his clients. Bob knows from experience that leadership is lonely, and he enjoys walking with his clients through the various challenges they face. He uses the leadership lessons he learned in the ministry along with the principles of *Core Motivator* to help his clients understand who they are and how to navigate their lives and businesses.

In 2006 he pursued his passion for wine and France and founded Art in a Glass. He travels to France every year and tastes hundreds of wines, selecting the best wines for his club members. His third book, *Defeated by Lunch*, is a collection of his favorite memories from his time in France (www.artinaglass.com).

In 2019 he became Executive Director of The Timothy Foundation, an organization committed to investing in the next generation of Christian leaders (www.thetimothyfoundation.com).

He is married to Debbie—his beautiful wife of over forty years—and they have two wonderful sons. The highlight of every year is the time he and Debbie spend in France discovering new places, meeting new friends, and enjoying fantastic food and wine.

He has a BA in economics from Roanoke College and a Masters of Divinity from Covenant Seminary.

End notes

1   I have purposely never read *Built to Last* for fear that some of what I write here might be accidentally borrowed from that work.